Time for Spanish

All it takes is twenty minutes a day

Robert Clarke

Stanley Thornes (Publishers) Ltd

First published in 1999 by:
Stanley Thornes (Publishers) Ltd
Ellenborough House
Wellington Street
CHELTENHAM GL50 1YW
England

A catalogue record for this book is available
from the British Library.

99 00 01 02 03 / 10 9 8 7 6 5 4 3 2 1

ISBN 0–7487–3875–4
ISBN 0–7487–3877–0 (complete pack)
ISBN 0–7487–3876–2 (cassettes)

Also available in the *Time for Languages* series:

Time for French, Paul Durrant
Time for German, Corinna Schicker
Time for Italian, Donatella de Ferra, Marina Mozzon-McPherson
Time for Portuguese, Sue Tyson-Ward

Cover: Joanna Kerr

Typeset by Action Publishing Technology Limited, Gloucester
Recorded at Matinée Sound & Vision, Reading
Voice artists: Marisa Julián, Mariluz Rodrigo, Imanol Guillen
Printed and bound in Great Britain by T. J. International Ltd, Padstow, Cornwall

How to make the best use of *Time for Spanish*

The material in *Time for Spanish* has been designed for you to complete one unit every day, but you are in control. If you want to cover several units in a day, then do that. Do try, however, to stick to a sensible routine so that you cover a number of units spread over the course of one week, rather than ten sessions at the weekend. You will retain so much more if you 'drip-feed' yourself. You should ideally work through the units in sequence, but again, you are in control. Choose a method which suits you best.

Throughout the 60 units, there are plenty of opportunities to practise speaking Spanish. Start by listening to the **Vocabulario** (vocabulary) section on the recording and follow the words in your book. Listen carefully to the pronunciation and try to mimic it as best you can yourself. There is space on the recording for you to repeat the word immediately after the actor. If possible, practise out loud, and don't be shy! The more you get used to hearing your own voice speaking Spanish, the easier it will become. The vocabulary is read out on the cassette until Unit 20. In the later units you can still practise reading the words and phrases out loud; you can check your pronunciation when you listen to the dialogues.

Now listen to the **Diálogo** (dialogue) section, first of all without following the transcript in the book, and then using the text. This uses the words you have been practising already. See how much you can understand before you consult the text. Don't worry if there are parts you miss – just try to catch the drift of what is said.

Once you have read through the text and unravelled its contents you are ready for the exercises. Some of these involve the recording, some don't. In Exercise 3 of some units you will be asked to take part in a speaking activity. Usually this takes the form of a dialogue with an actor on the recording. You will be given prompts in English on the recording, written in the book or by means of pictures. Make sure you follow the sequence of these prompts carefully to guide you in your responses. You will soon get used to the method used here, and you will find it invaluable in gaining confidence in speaking naturally.

Finally read the **Lenguaje** (usually a grammar hint) and **La vida española**, which gives you some background on the culture and lifestyle of Spanish-speaking Europe.

Do come back to units in the future to refresh your memory. Once you have covered the unit with the help of the book, you will find that playing the recordings in your car or while ironing, or whatever, will prove invaluable.

Good luck and enjoy learning Spanish!

Contents

My family and I

Introducing yourself formally

Vocabulario básico

primero/a	first
buenos días	good morning
pase	come in
¿es usted?	are you?
sí	yes
la señora ...	Mrs, the lady (ñ – as in o*ni*on)
¿quién?	who?
soy	I am
el señor	Mr, the gentleman
inglés (m); **inglesa** (f)	English
¿de dónde?	from where?
¿de qué parte?	from which part?
Inglaterra	England
la capital	the capital
la señorita	Miss, the young lady
siéntese	sit down

Diálogo

Mujer	Pase.
Hombre	Buenos días. ¿Es usted la señora Pérez?
Mujer	Sí, soy la señora Pérez. ¿Quién es usted?
Hombre	Soy el señor Smith.
Mujer	¿De dónde es usted?
Hombre	Soy inglés.
Mujer	Y, ¿de qué parte de Inglaterra es usted?
Hombre	Soy de Londres, la capital.
Mujer	Muy bien, señor Smith. Siéntese.

Ejercicios (Exercises)

(*Answers begin on page 126.*)

1 Fill in the speech bubbles. The people are giving their name and saying where they are from.

2 On the recording three people are giving their name and saying where they are from. Fill in the grid below.

Speaker	Name	Town of origin
1. Señor.	~~Señor~~ Silla.	Madrid.
2. Señora.	~~Señora~~ Blanco	Malaga.
3. Señorita.	~~Señorita~~ Perez.	Spain (Spanish).

3 Now take part in a dialogue, using the English prompts on the recording to help you. You can check your responses in the answers if necessary (*page 126*).

* Soy el Señor Pratside s.; * Si soy Ingles. * Soy de Londres, la capital.

Lenguaje (Language notes)

The word for 'I' is **Yo**, but it is rarely used. To identify yourself, you simply say: **Soy el señor/la señora/la señorita** + your name.

Usted is the word for 'you' in formal language, that is the language used to speak to people in authority, strangers, etc.

Adjectives of nationality change according to the gender of the speaker and are not written with a capital letter. For example:

Soy español.	I am Spanish. (*a male speaker*)
Soy española.	I am Spanish. (*a female speaker*)
Soy inglés.	I am English. (*a male speaker*)
Soy inglesa.	I am English. (*a female speaker*)

La vida española (Spanish life)

Mr, Mrs and Miss are considered to be formal titles and, when you give your name formally, you put **el** or **la** before the word **señor**, **señora** or **señorita**.

For example: **Soy la señora Pérez.**

However, when you address someone directly in a formal setting you do not use **el** or **la**.

For example: **Buenos días, señor Sala.**

In the hotel

Checking into a hotel room

Vocabulario básico

segundo/a	second
buenas tardes	good afternoon, good evening
tengo	I have
una habitación	a room (*'h' is always silent*)
reservada	reserved, booked (*of a feminine thing*)
aquí	here
su nombre	your name
por favor	please
eso es	that's so, right
individual	single
doble	double
con baño	with a bath
con ducha	with a shower
¿para cuántos días?	for how many days?
un(o)	one
dos	two
tres días	three days
cuatro	four
cinco	five (*Note: c + i, e = th as in 'thin'*)
seis	six
siete	seven
el piso	the floor, the flat or apartment
gracias	thank you

Diálogo

Cliente	Buenas tardes.
Recepcionista	Buenas tardes, señor.
Cliente	Tengo reservada una habitación aquí.
Recepcionista	¿Su nombre, por favor?
Cliente	Soy el señor Smith.
Recepcionista	¡Ah, sí! El señor Smith de Londres en Inglaterra.
Cliente	Eso es.
Recepcionista	¿Una habitación individual o doble?
Cliente	Doble, por favor.
Recepcionista	¿Con baño o con ducha?
Cliente	Con baño.
Recepcionista	Y, ¿para cuántos días?
Cliente	Para tres días.
Recepcionista	Muy bien. La habitación número siete en el primer piso.
Cliente	Gracias.

Ejercicios

1 Match the words to the pictures, writing down the number of the picture and the letter of the word. (*Answers on page 126.*)

1.

2.

3.

4.

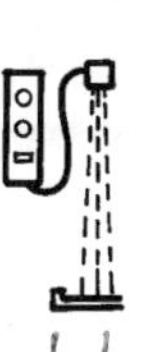

5.

6.

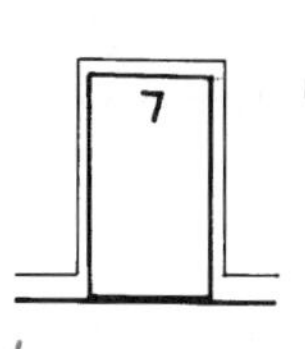

Words 1d. 2a. 3f. 4e 5c 6b.

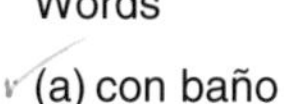

(a) con baño
(b) habitación número siete
(c) el hotel
(d) una habitación individual
(e) con ducha
(f) una habitación doble

2 On the recording two people are booking hotel rooms. Listen to the tape, and write down what they require.

Customer	Single/Double	Bath/Shower	No. of nights	Room no.
1. Losada.	individual.	con ducha.	cinco.	seis. (6)
2. Perez.	doble.	con bano.	seis	cuatro (4)

3 What would you say, in Spanish, to obtain the following in a Spanish hotel:

a) A single room with a bath for three days una habitación individual con bano para tres dias.
b) A double room with a shower for two days. una habitación doble. con ducha para dos dias.
c) A single room with a shower for six days. una habitación individual. con ducha para seis dias.

Lenguaje

All nouns in Spanish are either masculine or feminine. As a working rule, nouns ending in **-o** are masculine – **el libro**, 'the book', and those ending in **a** are feminine – **la casa**, 'the house'. With nouns that end in something else, such as **la habitación**, 'the room', you should learn the gender as you learn the noun.

Questions in Spanish begin with an inverted question mark – **¿** and end with a normal question mark – **?**

La vida española

There are various types of hotel in Spain. The best are converted castles or monasteries, and these are called **paradores**. The next category are **hoteles**, which are like large hotels the world over. **Hostales** offer rather fewer facilities than **hoteles** and are cheaper. **Pensiones** are similar to boarding houses in England. All hotels are classified according to a five-star system with the best having five stars.

My home town

Describing your home town

Vocabulario básico

tercero/a	third
está	is
el norte	the north
el este	the east
el sur	the south
el oeste	the west
el centro	the centre
cerca (de)	near (to)
¿cómo es ...?	how is it? (what's it like?)
grande	big
pequeño/a	small
bastante	rather, fairly
¿qué hay ...?	what is there?
el interés	the interest
para	for
el/la turista	the tourist
la catedral	the cathedral
el museo	the museum
la casa	the house
El Greco	El Greco (*16th/17th-century artist*)
¡qué ...!	how ...!
interesante	interesting

Diálogo

Hombre inglés	¿De dónde es usted, señora?
Mujer española	Soy de Toledo.
Hombre inglés	¿Dónde está Toledo?
Mujer española	Está en el centro de España, cerca de Madrid.
Hombre inglés	Y, ¿cómo es Toledo, grande o pequeña?
Mujer española	Es bastante grande.
Hombre inglés	¿Qué hay de interés en Toledo para los turistas?
Mujer española	Pues, hay la catedral, la Casa del Greco, el Museo del Greco ...
Hombre inglés	¡Qué interesante!

a) Madrid
b) Bilbao
c) Málaga
d) Valencia
e) Badajoz

Ejercicios

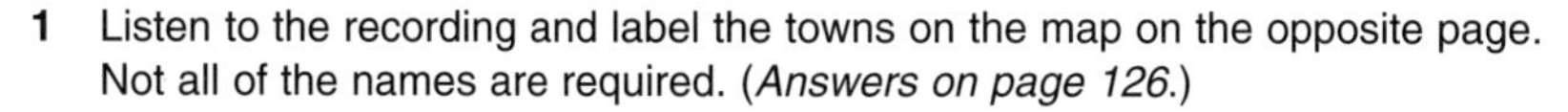

1 Listen to the recording and label the towns on the map on the opposite page. Not all of the names are required. (*Answers on page 126.*)

2 On the recording, two people are describing their home town. Fill in the grid below giving the details required.

Town	Position	Tourist interest
1.		
2.		

3 Take part in a dialogue, using the English prompts on the recording to help you. You can check your responses in the Answers (page 126) if necessary.

Lenguaje

To form the plural of nouns in Spanish you follow two simple rules. If the noun ends in a vowel, you add an **-s** to the noun: **la casa = las casas**. If the noun ends in a consonant, you add **-es** to the noun: **la catedral = las catedrales**. You therefore hear and see the plural form.

The verb **estar**, 'to be' is used to indicate position.

¿Dónde está la catedral? Where is the cathedral?

The verb **ser**, 'to be' is used to indicate permanent conditions.

Soy profesor. I am a teacher. (*permanently*)
Es español. He is Spanish. (*permanently*)

La vida española

The whole of Toledo has been declared a national monument. Therefore nothing n the town can be changed without reference to the Fine Arts Commission. This means that if you look at El Greco's paintings in the El Greco Museum, which portray the town as it was in the sixteenth century, you will find that the panorama of Toledo has not changed since that time.

Finding your way

Finding your way in a strange town

Vocabulario básico

cuarto/a	fourth
el/la transeúnte	the passerby
perdón	excuse me
¿por dónde se va a . . . ?	how does one get to . . . ?
el banco	the bank
el cine	the cinema
el sol	the sun
por aquí	around here
este/esta	this
la calle	the street
mire usted	look (*command*)
vaya por	go along (*command*)
tome	take (*command*)
a la derecha	on the right
a la izquierda	on the left (*'z' is always pronounced 'th'*)
al final de	at the end of
al lado de	beside, at the side of
ese/esa	that
lejos (de)	far (from) (*'j' as 'ch' in 'loch'*)
abierto/a	open
cien metros	100 metres
muchas gracias	thank you very much
de nada	don't mention it

Diálogo

Turista	Perdón, señor, ¿por dónde se va al Banco Popular?
Transeúnte	Vaya por esta calle y tome la primera calle a la derecha y luego la segunda a la izquierda. El Banco Popular está en esa calle al lado del Cine Sol.
Turista	¿Está lejos?
Transeúnte	No. Está bastante cerca.
Turista	Y. ¿Está abierto el banco ahora?
Transeúnte	Sí, está abierto.
Turista	Muchas gracias.
Transeúnte	De nada, señora.

Ejercicios

1 Look at the town plan on the opposite page. Listen to the three sets of instructions given on the recording and write down the name of the building to which you are being directed each time. (*Answers on page 126.*)

1. ______________ 2. ______________ 3. ______________

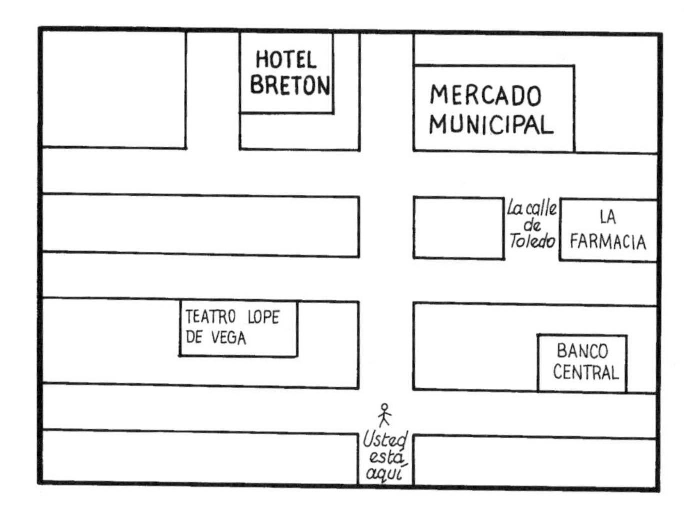

2 On the recording, two people are asking for directions. Fill in the grid below in English, giving the building they are looking for and how they will get there.

Building	Directions given
1.	
2.	

3 Recreate the dialogue on the facing page, using the prompts below. You are asking the way to the Banco Central. Look at the Answers (*page 126*) if you need help.

- You ask a passerby: 'Where is the Banco Central?'
- You ask if it is far.
- You ask if it's open.

Lenguaje

Commands found in this lesson are as follows: **Mire usted** — 'look'; **vaya** — 'go'; **tome** — 'take'. The word for 'you', **usted**, is often missed out after the first order in a series.

There are words which join up to form new words. After **a**, 'to', and **de**, 'from', the word for 'the' with masculine nouns changes: **a + el = al**; **de + el = del**.

Vaya al banco.	Go to the bank.
Está cerca del mercado.	It's near the market.

La vida española

When asking for directions in Spanish you must use the formal phrase: **¿Por dónde se va a** (+ name of the building)**?** If you ask the simple question: **¿Dónde está el Hotel Breton?**, the Spanish speaker may simply say: **En la calle de Toledo**, because you asked where the hotel is and he has told you!

Goods and services

Changing traveller's cheques

Vocabulario básico

quinto/a	fifth
querer	to wish; to want
quiero	I want, wish
¿quiere usted?	do you want?
cambiar	to change
el cheque de viaje	the traveller's cheque
la libra (esterlina)	the pound
el dólar	the dollar
¿cuánto/a/os/as?	how much, many
ocho	eight
veinte	twenty
treinta	thirty
cuarenta	forty
cincuenta	fifty
¿quiere usted firmar?	Will you sign? (*polite request*)
claro	of course
el pasaporte	the passport
aquí tiene usted	here you are (*literally, 'here you have it'*)
la ventanilla	the bank counter (*pronounce 'll' as in 'million'*)
el dinero	the money

Diálogo

Turista	Quiero cambiar unos cheques de viaje, por favor.
Empleada	Muy bien. ¿Son libras esterlinas o dólares?
Turista	Libras esterlinas.
Empleada	¿Cuántas libras quiere usted cambiar?
Turista	Veinte libras.
Empleada	¿Quiere usted firmar los cheques?
Turista	Sí, claro.
Empleada	¿Tiene usted su pasaporte?
Turista	Sí. Aquí tiene usted.
Empleada	Gracias. Vaya a la ventanilla número cinco para el dinero.
Turista	Gracias.

Ejercicios

1 Say aloud these simple sums. Example: 1 + 1 = 2 **Uno y uno son dos.** (*Answers on page 126.*)

(a) 2 + 2 = 4
(b) 3 + 2 = 5
(c) 4 + 2 = 6
(d) 3 + 4 = 7
(e) 5 + 3 = 8

2 On the recording two people are changing money in a bank. Fill in the grid below to show how much money they wish to change and which cash desk they are directed to.

Customer	Currency	Amount	Cash desk
1.			
2.			

3 Unscramble the following sentence to form the basic sentences required to change travellers' cheques in Spain.

a) Por cheques cambiar unos viaje quiero favor de.
b) Cuarenta quiero dólares cambiar.
c) Mi aquí pasaporte usted tiene.

Lenguaje

The question word **¿Cuánto?** agrees with the noun it precedes.

¿Cuántas libras tiene usted?	How many pounds do you have? (*feminine and plural*)
¿Cuántos dólares quiere usted cambiar?	How many dollars do you want to change? (*masculine and plural*)

La vida española

Not all banks in Spain change foreign currency, and you should look for one which displays the sign **Cambio**.

Banks are usually open from 9 a.m. to 2 p.m. on Mondays to Fridays and 9 a.m. to 12.30 p.m. on Saturdays. Most banks now have cash dispensers which accept international credit cards.

Food and drink

Getting a snack in a café

Vocabulario básico

sexto/a	sixth
¿qué va usted a tomar?	what are you going to have? (*food and drink*)
un café solo	a black coffee
un café con leche	a white coffee
una cerveza	a beer
una naranjada	an orangeade
un limón natural	a fresh lemon juice
algo	something
¿algo para comer?	something to eat?
¿qué tiene usted?	what do you have?
¿qué tiene usted para comer?	what do you have to eat?
un sandwich	a sandwich
un bocadillo	a filled bread roll
un bollo	a bun
tráigame	bring me (*order*)
el queso	the cheese
el tomate	the tomato
el jamón	the ham
en seguida	right away, at once

Diálogo

Camarero Buenas tardes. ¿Qué va usted a tomar?
Cliente Un café con leche.
Camarero ¿Algo para comer?
Cliente ¿Qué tiene usted para comer?
Camarero Pues, hay bocadillos, sandwiches, bollo ...
Cliente Tráigame un sandwich de queso y tomate.
Camarero Un café con leche y un sandwich de queso y tomate.
Cliente Eso es.
Camarero En seguida, señorita.

Ejercicios

1 Match up the pictures to the labels by writing down the number of the picture and the letter of the label.

1. 
2. 
3. 
4. 

5. 

(a) Una naranjada (b) Un café solo (c) Una cerveza (d) Un limón natural
(e) Un café con leche

________ ________ ________ ________ ________

2 On the recording three people are ordering something in a café. Write down what each one orders.

(a) ____________ (b) ____________ (c) ____________

3 Recreate the dialogue on the facing page, using the visual cues to help you. Look at the Answers (*page 126*) if you need help.

1.

2.

3.

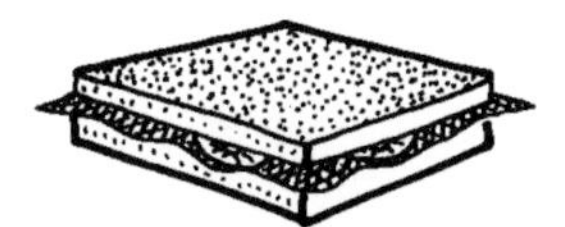

4.

Lenguaje

Tráigame, 'bring me', allows you to order drinks, snacks and meals in a bar or restaurant.

Tráigame un café solo.	Bring me a black coffee.
Tráigame un sandwich de bacón y tomate.	Bring me a bacon and tomato sandwich.

The verb **comer**, 'to eat', is regular, which means it follows a simple pattern.

Como ***en casa.***	I eat at home.
Comes en un bar.	You eat in a bar. (*talking to a friend*)
Come en un restaurante.	He/She eats in a restaurant.
Usted come en una cafetería.	You eat in a cafeteria. (*talking to a stranger*)

Most verbs which end in **-er** follow this pattern.

La vida española

Bars and cafés in Spain have two prices for each item they sell. One is for being served sitting at a table (**mesa**), and the other for standing or sitting at the bar (**barra**), and the latter is cheaper. Therefore, if you follow the English custom in a pub of getting your drink at the bar and then sitting at a table, you will offend local customs. **Un sandwich** is usually toasted, and **un bocadillo** is a bread roll with a filling of cheese, ham, etc.

Travel

Ordering tickets in a railway station

Vocabulario básico

séptimo/a	seventh
la estación de ferrocarril	the railway station
el taquillero	the booking office clerk
la hora	the hour, the time
¿a qué hora?	at what time?
salir	to leave, go out, depart (*Note:* **salgo** = 'I go out')
el tren	the train
próximo/a	next
para	for, destined for
a las nueve	at 9 o'clock
a las nueve y diez	at ten past nine
a las nueve y cuarto	at a quarter past nine
a las nueve y media	at half past nine
a las diez menos cuarto	at a quarter to ten
el billete	the ticket (*travel*), the note (*money*)
de ida	single
de ida y vuelta	return
la clase	class
la peseta	the peseta
mil	thousand (*invariable*)
el andén	platform
la vía	track
la viajera	traveller (*female*)

Diálogo

Viajera	Buenos días. ¿A qué hora sale el próximo tren para Madrid?
Taquillero	Sale a las nueve y media.
Viajera	Dos billetes, por favor.
Taquillero	¿De ida y vuelta o sólo de ida?
Viajera	De ida y vuelta.
Taquillero	¿De qué clase, primera o segunda?
Viajera	De segunda.
Taquillero	Aquí tiene usted. Son dos mil pesetas.
Viajera	Gracias. ¿De dónde sale el tren?
Taquillero	Andén número cinco. Por allí y a la izquierda.

Ejercicios

1 What would you say to get these tickets?

Examples:

= **Un billete de ida, segunda clase para Barcelona.**

= **Un billete de ida y vuelta, primera clase para Sevilla.**

2 On the recording three people are buying rail tickets. Note down on the grid what each one wants.

Number of tickets	Class	Single/Return	Destination
1.			
2.			
3.			

3 Recreate the dialogue on the facing page, using the written cues below to help you. (*Answers on page 126.*)

- Ask what time the next train to Barcelona leaves.
- You'd like two tickets, please.
- You'd like two singles.
- You want first class.
- You want to know which platform.

Lenguaje

The answer to the question **¿A qué hora ...?** begins with **A las** (+ time) or **A la** if the number one is involved.

A las diez.	At ten o'clock.
A las diez y cinco.	At five past ten.
A las diez y cuarto.	A a quarter past ten.
A las diez y media.	At half past ten.

After half past, you change to the next hour and deduct the amount of time as needed.

A las once menos cuarto.	At a quarter to eleven.
¿A qué hora sale el tren para Sevilla? A la una.	At one o'clock.

La vida española

The Spanish railway system is called '**la Renfe**'. The principal types of train are:
AVE – a high-speed train like the French TGV.
Intercity – similar to the British train of the same name.
Talgo – a fast long-distance train.
Electrotren – a fast electric train.
Rápido, **expreso** – a night, stopping train.
Tren de cercanías – similar to a British commuter train.

Free time

Hobbies and free time

Vocabulario básico

octavo/a	eighth
¿qué hace usted?	what do you do?
el tiempo	the time (*also* the weather – *see Unit 9*)
practico	I play
el tenis	tennis
¿practica usted?	do you play?
alguno/a	some, a
el deporte	the sport
el golf	golf
mi, mis	my
el marido	the husband
el hijo	the son
el fútbol	football
el colegio	school
también	also
es aficionado a	he's keen on
la novela	the novel
el libro	the book
histórico/a	historical

Diálogo

Mujer	¿Qué hace usted en su tiempo libre?
Hombre	Practico el tenis. ¿Practica usted algún deporte?
Mujer	Sí. Practico el golf con mi marido.
Hombre	¿Y su hijo? ¿Practica algún deporte?
Mujer	Sí. Practica el fútbol en el colegio. También es muy aficionado a las novelas históricas.

Ejercicios

1 Complete the following sentences using the appropriate option from the list below.

1. ¿Practica ______ el tenis?
2. Mi marido practica _______.
3. Es aficionado a _____________________.
4. El hijo practica el fútbol _____________.

(a) en el colegio
(b) usted
(c) el golf
(d) las novelas históricas

2 On the recording four people are talking about their leisure activities. Select what each one does from the list below:

1. (a) Golf (b) Football (c) Tennis
2. (a) Tennis (b) Football (c) Golf
3. (a) Football (b) Tennis (c) Golf
4. (a) Keen on books (b) Keen on golf (c) Keen on tennis

3 Recreate the dialogue on the facing page, using the written cues to help you. (*Answers on page 126.*)

- You are talking to a friend. Tell her you play football.
- Ask whether your friend plays some sport.
- Say that your son plays tennis at school.
- He also likes books.

Lenguaje

Most verbs in Spanish follow a simple, regular pattern and are classified according to their endings into **-ar**, **-er** and **-ir** verbs.

-ar		**-er**		**-ir**	
Practicar	to play	**Comer**	to eat	**Escribir**	to write
practico	I play	**como**	I eat	**escribo**	I write
practicas	you play*	**comes**	you eat*	**escribes**	you write*
practica	he/she plays	**come**	he/she eats	**escribe**	he/she writes
usted practica	you play	**usted come**	you eat	**usted escribe**	you write

*This form, the 2nd person singular, is used to speak to family, friends, children and animals.

La vida española

Nowadays Spain is well provided with leisure facilities. Many fine golf courses, tennis clubs and water parks are found in the south. Skiing is available in the Pyrenees in the north, at Navacerrada near Madrid and in the Sierra Nevada in the south. Because of the changes in altitude at this latter location it is possible to ski in the morning, drop down to sea level and bathe in the sea in the afternoon.

The weather

What's the weather like?

Vocabulario básico

noveno/a	ninth	**enero**	January
el tiempo	the weather	**febrero**	February
¿qué tiempo hace?	what's the weather like?	**marzo**	March
siempre	always	**abril**	April
hace buen tiempo	the weather is fine	**mayo**	May
hace mal tiempo	the weather is bad	**junio**	June
hace sol	it's sunny	**julio**	July
hace calor	it's hot	**agosto**	August
hace frío	it's cold	**setiembre**	September
todo	all	**octubre**	October
pero	but	**noviembre**	November
el verano	the summer	**diciembre**	December
el invierno	the winter	**el año**	the year
		hoy	today
		¿verdad?	true? is that right? etc. (*see Lenguaje*)

Diálogo

Turista Hace buen tiempo hoy, ¿verdad?
Camarero Sí, siempre hace sol en Madrid en el verano.
Turista Y, hace calor también, ¿no?
Camarero Claro. En julio y agosto hace mucho calor.
Turista ¿Hace frío aquí en el invierno?
Camarero Sí, señora, hace mal tiempo y también hace mucho frío. En Inglaterra hace mal tiempo todo el año, ¿verdad?
Turista Bueno. En el invierno hace mal tiempo y hace frío, pero en el verano hace sol.
Camarero ¿Qué va a tomar, señora?
Turista Un café con leche.

Ejercicios

1 Match the captions to the pictures, writing down the number of the picture and the letter of the caption.

1. 

2. 

3. 

4. 

5. 

(a) Hace sol.
(b) Hace buen tiempo.
(c) Hace frío.
(d) Hace mal tiempo.
(e) Hace calor.

2 On the recording four people are discussing the weather. Fill in the grid below to show what the weather is like in their region.

1. Madrid
2. Pyrenees
3. Seville
4. N. Spain

3 Answer the questions on the recording, using the visual clues below to help you. (*Answers on page 126.*)

Lenguaje

To ask what the weather is like you use the question: **¿Qué tiempo hace?** Many of the answers begin **Hace** (+ a noun). Literally you are saying: **Hace sol** = 'It makes sun'. You can use **mucho** to modify the noun: **Hace mucho sol** = 'It is very sunny'.

¿verdad? enables you to turn any statement into a question:

Es inglés.	He's English.
Es inglés, ¿verdad?	He's English, isn't he?

Months of the year are always written with a small letter.

Voy a Sevilla el tres de abril.	I'm going to Seville on the third of April.

La vida española

In the centre of Spain the climate is known as 'continental': long, hard winters and short, very hot summers. Spring and autumn hardly exist, and the change from summer to winter and from winter to summer is very brusque. The weather is summed up in the Spanish saying: **Nueve meses de invierno y tres de infierno.** (Nine months of winter and three of Hell.)

Unit 10 Numbers

Giving your telephone number

Vocabulario básico

décimo/a	tenth	**cinco**	five
cero	zero, nought	**seis**	six
uno	one	**siete**	seven
dos	two	**ocho**	eight
tres	three	**nueve**	nine
cuatro	four	**diez**	ten
once	eleven	**dieciséis**	sixteen
doce	twelve	**diecisiete**	seventeen
trece	thirteen	**dieciocho**	eighteen
catorce	fourteen	**diecinueve**	nineteen
quince	fifteen		
veinte	twenty	**treinta**	thirty
veintidós	twenty-two	**treinta y ocho**	thirty-eight
cuarenta	forty	**cincuenta**	fifty
cuarenta y cinco	forty-five	**cincuenta y uno**	fifty-one
sesenta	sixty	**setenta**	seventy
sesenta y seis	sixty-six	**setenta y cuatro**	seventy-four
ochenta	eighty	**noventa**	ninety
ochenta y nueve	eighty-nine	**noventa y siete**	ninety-seven
cien	one hundred (*exactly* 100)		
ciento dieciséis	one hundred and sixteen		

Diálogo

Mujer ¿Cuál es su número de teléfono?
Hombre En Inglaterra es cero, uno, nueve, cero, cuatro, siete, seis, nueve, seis, cero, ocho.
Mujer Y, ¿aquí en Madrid?
Hombre Estoy en el Hotel Moderno. El número de teléfono es cinco, treinta y uno, sesenta y cinco, veinte.
Mujer Y, ¿el número de la habitación?
Hombre Estoy en la habitación número ochenta y seis.
Mujer Gracias.
Hombre ¿Cuál es su número de teléfono?
Mujer Es el cinco, cuarenta y uno, setenta y dos, veintisiete.
Hombre Gracias.

Ejercicios

1 Match the figures inside the circle with the words outside. Be careful! Not all of the words are needed. (*Answers on pages 126–7.*)

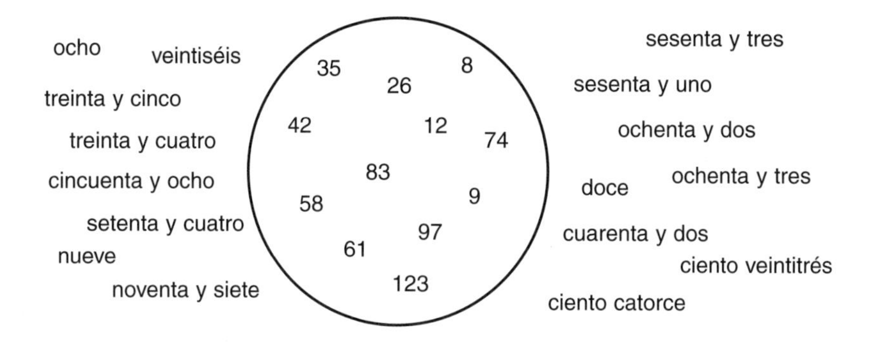

2 On the recording three people are giving their telephone numbers. Select the correct one from the three given below for each number.

1. (a) 2, 70, 96, 51 (b) 2, 60, 96, 51 (c) 2, 36, 96, 45.
2. (a) 2, 53, 76, 32 (b) 2, 24, 94, 31 (c) 2, 54, 65, 32.
3. (a) 5, 65, 13, 87 (b) 5, 55, 12, 83 (c) 6, 55, 15, 75.

3 Say aloud the following sums. For example: 25 + 25 = 50
Veinticinco y veinticinco son cincuenta.
a) 45 + 55 = 100. b) 21 + 12 = 33. c) 64 + 22 = 86
d) 35 + 38 = 73 e) 52 + 17 = 69

Lenguaje

Numbers are written as one word from 1 to 29. After that they are written as three words: 35 – **treinta y cinco**. The number for 100, **ciento**, shortens to **cien** when you refer to exactly 100.

Hay cien casas en el pueblo. There are 100 houses in the village.

To practice numbers you can use familiar objects such as car number plates. Say the number to yourself as the car approaches – M 984 BUA = **nueve ocho cuatro**. You can also count street lamps as you pass, first as simple numbers, **uno, dos, tres**, and then in multiples, **dos, cuatro, seis, ocho**, etc.

La vida española

Telephone numbers in Spain are given in pairs unless the first number contains three numbers, and then a digit is used. Therefore 261 27 42 is given as: **Dos, sesenta y uno, veintisiete, cuarenta y dos**.

UNIT 5 Emergencies

Reclaiming lost property

Vocabulario básico

vamos a ver	let's see
el bolso	the handbag, bag
¿de qué es?	what is it made of?
de tela	made of fabric
de piel	made of leather
de plástico	made of plastic
¿de qué color es?	what colour is it?
verde	green
azul	blue
las gafas de sol	sunglasses
la tarjeta de crédito	the credit card
¿algo más?	anything else?
la bufanda	the scarf

Diálogo

Empleado	Vamos a ver, señora. Un bolso, ¿verdad?
Turista	Sí, un bolso.
Empleado	Y, ¿cómo es el bolso, grande o pequeño?
Turista	Pues, es bastante pequeño.
Empleado	¿De qué es? ¿Es de plástico, de tela o de piel?
Turista	Es de tela.
Empleado	¿De qué color es?
Turista	Es verde y azul.
Empleado	¿Qué hay en el bolso, señora?
Turista	Pues, hay unas tarjetas de crédito ...
Empleado	¿Algo más?
Turista	Sí. Hay unas gafas de sol y una bufanda.
Empleado	Pues, éste es su bolso, señora.
Turista	Muchas gracias.

Ejercicios

1 Match the captions to the pictures, discover which picture does not have a caption and write it down here ____________________ . (*Answers on p.127.*)

1.

2.

3.

4.

5.

Captions: (a) una bufanda (b) dinero español (c) una gafas de sol (d) una tarjeta de crédito.

2 On the recording three people are reclaiming lost property. Fill in the grid below, giving all the details.

Thing claimed	Size	Colour	Made of	Contents
1.				
2.				
3.				

3 Fill in the gaps to reclaim a small, green, leather handbag from a Lost Property Office.

– Un bolso, ¿verdad? ¿Cómo es el bolso?..
– ¿De qué color es?..
– ¿De qué es?..
– Entonces, éste es su bolso.

Lenguaje

The word for 'a', 'an' (the indefinite article) is **un**, **una** in Spanish, depending on whether the object is masculine or feminine, and the plural form is **unos**, **unas**. The plural form is not as widely used in Spanish as in English.

To ask what an object is like, you use the question: **¿Cómo es ...?**; to ask what colour it is, you use **¿De qué color es ...?**, and to ask what something is made of, you say: **¿De qué es ...?**

¿Cómo es? **Es grande.**	What's it like? It's big.
¿De qué color es? **Es gris.**	What colour is it? It's grey.
¿De qué es? **Es de tela.**	What's it made of? It's made of cloth.

La vida española

If you are unfortunate enough to lose something of value when in Spain, you go to the **Oficina de objetos perdidos** (Lost Property Office) of the company concerned. Theft from cars, and particularly from cars with a foreign number plate, is not uncommon. If this happens to you, go to the local **Comisaría** (Police Station) to make a complaint (**una denuncia**). You will need a police report of the incident for your insurance company back home.

My family and I

Talking about your family

Vocabulario básico

casado/a	married
¿está usted casado?	are you married?
estoy	I am
el arquitecto	the architect
el hijo	the son
la hija	the daughter
¿cómo se llaman?	what are they called?
¿cuántos años tienen?	how old are they?
veintiuno (veintiún)	twenty-one (**veintiún** *before a masculine singular noun*)
¿trabajan?	do they work?
¿estudian?	do they study?
la oficina	the office
la compañía	the company
el seguro	the insurance
el/la estudiante	the student
la universidad	the university
la alumna	the pupil (*female*)

Diálogo

Hombre	¿Está usted casada, doña Isabel?
Mujer	Sí, estoy casada. Mi marido es arquitecto.
Hombre	¿Tiene usted hijos?
Mujer	Sí, tengo dos: un hijo y una hija.
Hombre	¿Cómo se llaman?
Mujer	El hijo se llama Paco y la hija se llama Ana.
Hombre	¿Cuántos años tienen?
Mujer	Paco tiene veintiún años y Ana diecinueve.
Hombre	¿Estudian o trabajan?
Mujer	Paco trabaja en la oficina de una compañía de seguros, y Ana es estudiante en la Universidad de Madrid. ¿Tiene usted hijos, don Manuel?
Hombre	Sí. Tengo una hija. Tiene doce años y es alumna en el Colegio Galdós.

Ejercicios

1 Follow the lines and say how old each person is. For example: **Pilar tiene cinco años**. (*Answers on page 127.*)

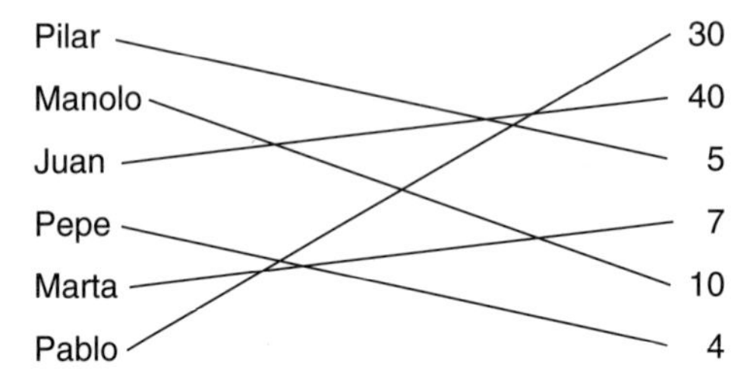

2 On the recording two people are talking about their family. Fill in the grid below giving the details listed.

Civil status	Children	Name/s	Age/s	Job/study
1.				
2.				

3 Give the following information, in Spanish, to your Spanish friend.

(a) I have one son. He's called Manuel, is twenty years old and is a student at the university.

(b) I have 2 children; a son and a daughter. They are called Pepe and Marta and are eighteen and twenty-two years old.

Lenguaje

When referring to your profession, you simply use the verb **ser** + the name of the profession without the indefinite article, **un** or **una**.

Soy profesor.	I'm a teacher.
Mi mujer es ama de casa.	My wife is a housewife.
Mi hijo es dentista.	My son is a dentist.
Mi hija es jefa de marketing.	My daughter is a marketing head.

To refer to sons *and* daughters, or parents, or brothers *and* sisters, you use the plural of the relevant *masculine* noun:
mis padres, 'my parents'; **mis hijos**, 'my sons and daughters'; **mis hermanos**, 'my brothers and sisters'. (In this regard Spanish is slightly sexist!)

La vida española

When using a person's surname, you address them as **señor Pérez**, **señora Sala** or **señorita Amodia**. If you know them well enough to use their first name but still wish to show respect, you use **don Pablo** or **doña Marta**. Young people or well established friends simply use the person's first name. **¡Hola, Paco! ¿Qué hay?** = Hello, Paco, How are things?

UNIT 13

In the hotel

Booking a room in a hotel

Vocabulario básico

poder	to be able, can
servir	to serve, help
¿en qué puedo servirle?	how can I help you?
libre	free
¿cuánto vale?	how much is it?
por día	per day
la comida	the meal, food, lunch
el desayuno	the breakfast
la cena	the dinner
cada	each, every (*invariable*)
la llave	the key
trescientas	300
lunes	Monday
martes	Tuesday
miércoles	Wednesday
jueves	Thursday
viernes	Friday
sábado	Saturday
domingo	Sunday

Diálogo

Recepcionista	Buenos días, señor. ¿En qué puedo servirle?
Cliente	¿Tiene una habitación libre?
Recepcionista	¿Individual o doble?
Cliente	Individual, por favor.
Recepcionista	¿Para cuántos días?
Cliente	Para tres días; hasta el domingo.
Recepcionista	Muy bien.
Cliente	¿Cuánto vale la habitación?
Recepcionista	Vale ocho mil pesetas por día.
Cliente	¿Y las comidas? ¿Cuánto valen?
Recepcionista	El desayuno vale trescientas pesetas, la comida y la cena valen dos mil trescientas cada una.
Cliente	Gracias.
Recepcionista	Habitación número veintitrés en el segundo piso. Aquí tiene usted la llave.

Ejercicios

1 Follow the lines and say aloud the various prices in this hotel.

1. La habitación	2.000 pesetas
2. El desayuno	2.300 pesetas
3. La comida	8.000 pesetas
4. La cena	300 pesetas

2 These are the answers, but, what were the questions?

(a) Doble, por favor
(b) Para cinco días
(c) Con baño
(d) Vale doce mil pesetas por día.

3 Recreate the dialogue on the facing page using the verbal cues to help you. (*Answers on page 127.*)

- Ask if she has a room free.
- Say 'A double room.'
- Say 'For five days, until Friday.'
- Ask the price of the room.
- Ask the price of the meals.
- Say 'Thank you'.

Lenguaje

The numbers 100–1,000 are as follows. (The irregular ones are underlined.)

100 – **ciento** (**cien** when exactly 100); **200** – **doscientos**; **300** – **trescientos**; **400** – **cuatrocientos**; <u>**500 – quinientos**</u>; **600** – **seiscientos**; <u>**700 – setecientos**</u>; **800** – **ochocientos**; <u>**900 – novecientos**</u>; **1.000 – mil** (invariable)

These numbers behave as adjectives, and agree with the noun.

800 boys – **ochocient*os* chic*os***.
800 girls – **ochocient*as* chic*as***.

The conjunction **y**, 'and', occurs between tens and units in large numbers: **2.795** – **Dos mil setecientas noventa *y* cinco**.

La vida española

The price you pay for most hotel rooms in Spain is for the room and *not* per person. If you go to the Tourist Office – **la Oficina de turismo** – in a Spanish town, the staff will give you a list of hotels and their prices for the area – **la lista de Hoteles**.

If you wish to register a formal complaint in a Spanish hotel, café or restaurant, you ask for the Complaints Book – **el libro de reclamaciones**. In Europe a full stop is used in numbers where we would use a comma, and a comma is used where we would use a full stop.

UNIT 14

My home town

Describing your home town

Vocabulario básico

exactamente	exactly
el pueblo	the village
la ciudad	the town, city
el/la habitante	the inhabitant
bonito/a	nice, pretty
antiguo/a	ancient, old
la plaza	the square
mayor	bigger, greater, main (*of street or square*)
el barrio	the district, area (*of town*)
industrial	industrial
la agricultura	agriculture
la región	the region (*pronounce 'gi' or 'ge' like 'ch' in 'loch'*)
la gente	the people
simpático/a	nice, pleasant (*of people*)

Diálogo

Hombre Usted es de Plasencia, ¿verdad?
Mujer Eso es.
Hombre Y, ¿dónde está Plasencia exactamente?
Mujer Está en Extremadura, cerca de Cáceres.
Hombre Y, ¿qué es, un pueblo o una ciudad?
Mujer Es una ciudad pequeña. Tiene cuarenta mil habitantes.
Hombre ¿Es una ciudad bonita?
Mujer El barrio antiguo con la Plaza Mayor y la catedral es muy bonito.
Hombre ¿Es una ciudad industrial?
Mujer No. Es el centro de la agricultura de la región.
Hombre ¿Es simpática la gente?
Mujer Sí, la gente es muy simpática.

Ejercicios

1 Look at the map of Spain, and answer the following questions aloud:

¿Dónde está Plasencia? ¿Y Carmona? ¿Y Chinchón? ¿Y Sabadell?

2 On the recording three people are talking about their home town. On the grid, write down what they tell you about it.

	Position in Spain	Type of town	Character of people
1. Carmona			
2. Chinchón			
3. Sabadell			

3 Unscramble the words in **bold** to give information about a Spanish town.

Está **crace** de **ridmad.** Tiene cuatro mil **bitteshana.** La catedral es muy **toniab.** La gente es muy **mápsicati.**

Lenguaje

Bonito is used to say something is 'nice' or 'pretty': **Es una ciudad muy bonita.** 'It's a very nice city.'

Guapo is used to say someone is pretty: **La hermana de Pedro es muy guapa.** 'Peter's sister is very pretty.'

Antiguo expresses 'old' of places or thing: **Es una ciudad muy antigua.** 'It's a very old city.'

Viejo can be used to say that people, places or things are 'old': **Tengo un coche muy viejo.** 'I've got a very old car.'

La vida española

Spain is now divided into seventeen autonomous regions, each with its regional government and flag. Spaniards are very proud of their home region – **la patria chica** – to the point that each town has a special noun for its inhabitants. Where do you think the following people are from? (The map will help you.) **Los madrileños**; **los sevillanos**; **los barceloneses**; **los granadinos**; **los valencianos**; **los alicantinos**. For the answers see page 127.

Finding your way

Finding your way to a hospital

Vocabulario básico

el hospital	the hospital
vaya	go (*order*)
¿va usted?	are you going?
todo derecho	straight ahead
hasta	as far as (*place*), until (*time*)
tuerza	turn (*order*)
el árbol	the tree
el coche	the car
el minuto	the minute
entonces	then
sólo	only

Diálogo

Turista	Perdón, señora, ¿hay un hospital en esta parte de la ciudad?
Transeúnte	Sí, señor. Hay un hospital en la Plaza Mayor.
Turista	Y, ¿por dónde se va a la Plaza Mayor?
Transeúnte	Vaya todo derecho hasta el final de la calle. Luego tuerza a la izquierda y tome la tercera calle a la derecha. La Plaza Mayor está al final de esa calle; es una plaza con muchos árboles.
Turista	¿Está lejos?
Transeúnte	¿Va usted en coche?
Turista	Sí.
Transeúnte	Entonces no está lejos. Sólo cinco minutos.
Turista	Gracias.

Ejercicios

1 Match the directional arrows to the captions, writing down the number of the direction and the letter of the caption.

1. 2.

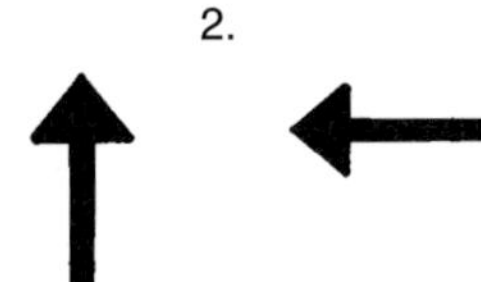

3.

4.

5.

(a) Tuerza a la derecha.
(b) El hospital está al final de la calle.
(c) Vaya todo derecho.
(d) Tuerza a la izquierda.
(e) Tome la primera calle a la derecha.

________ ________ ________ ________ ________

2 On the recording two people are asking for directions. On the grid note down what each is looking for and how they can get there.

Place sought	1st instruction	2nd instruction	3rd instruction
1.			
2.			

3 Recreate the dialogue on the facing page, using the English cues given below to help you. *(Answers on page 127.)*

- Say 'excuse me', and ask if there is a bank in this part of the town.
- Ask how you get there.
- Say yes, you have a car.
- Say thank you.

Lenguaje

The verb **ir**, 'to go', is irregular:

voy	I go, am going
vas	you go, are going (*informal*)
va	he/she goes, is going
usted va	you go, are going (*formal*)

The verb ***torcer*** changes the **o** to **ue** in all parts of the present singular and changes the **c** to **z** before **a** or **o**:

tuerzo	I turn
tuerces	you turn (*informal*)
tuerce	he/she turns
usted tuerce	you turn (*formal*)

The command form is *tuerza*, because it is formed from a 1st person singular, removing the **-o** and adding **-a**.

La vida española

Help with medical emergencies is available from several sources in Spain. Most hospitals have a **Centro de urgencias**, and help is also provided at the roadside by **Puestos de socorro** and **Puestos de primeros auxilios**. In town the chemist's (**la farmacia**) will offer help and advice, and outside of normal opening hours, each chemist's will direct you to the emergency chemist's – **la farmacia de guardia**.

Goods and services

In a market, buying food for a picnic

Vocabulario básico

el mercado	the market
el puesto	the market stall
la charcutería	the cooked meats (*and* shop)
desear	to want, wish
póngame	give me (*literally* 'put for me') (*order*)
el jamón de York	the cooked ham
¿eso es todo?	is that all?
trescientos/as	300
setecientos/as	700
la verdulería	the greengrocer's
la lechuga	the lettuce
los comestibles	groceries
déme	give me (*order*)
la botella	the bottle
el panecillo	the bread roll
las patatas fritas	the crisps, chips (*in a restaurant*)
el agua mineral	mineral water
con gas	sparkling, fizzy
sin gas	still

Diálogos

En la charcutería

Vendedora	Buenos días. ¿Qué desea?
Hombre	Póngame un cuarto de kilo de jamón de York.
Vendedora	Aquí tiene usted. ¿Algo más?
Hombre	Sí. Medio kilo de ese queso.
Vendedora	¿Eso es todo?
Hombre	Sí ¿Cuánto es todo?
Vendedora	Son setecientas pesetas, señor.

En la verdulería

Vendedora	¿Qué desea?
Hombre	Déme una lechuga y medio kilo de tomates.
Vendedora	Aquí tiene usted. Son trescientas pesetas.

En el puesto de comestibles

Vendedora	¿Qué desea, señor?
Hombre	Déme seis panecillos y una botella de agua mineral.
Vendedora	¿Con gas o sin gas?
Hombre	Con gas.
Vendedora	Aquí tiene usted. Son ciento cincuenta pesetas.

Ejercicios

1 Compare the shopping with the shopping list, and write down what the shopper forgot to buy. ___

2 On the recording two people are shopping in a market. Mark the following statements TRUE or FALSE.

1. She buys a kilo of cheese and a quarter of York ham. ___
2. She buys two kilos of tomatoes and two lettuces. ___

3 Recreate the dialogues on the facing page, using the following cues to help you. (*Answers on page 127.*)

- Ask for ½ kilo of ham.
- Yes, a kilo of cheese.
- Say yes. Ask how much it all is.
- Ask for two lettuces and a kilo of tomatoes.
- Ask her to give you four bread rolls and a bottle of mineral water.
- You want still water.

Lenguaje

Póngame is used to ask for things when a certain element of weighing, measuring or preparing is involved.

Póngame un café con leche.	Give me a white coffee.
Póngame dos kilos de tomates.	Give me two kilos of tomatoes.
Póngame veinte litros de gasolina.	Give me 20 litres of petrol.

Déme expresses 'give me' when you are asking for goods already packed or where no measurement is involved.

Déme dos lechugas.	Give me two lettuces.
Déme un paquete de café.	Give me a packet of coffee.

La vida española

The best, and often cheapest, place to buy food in Spain is in the local market. The quality of the produce is normally high, competition ensures that the prices are low, and the good humour of the stallkeepers ensures that a visit to the market is always a lively event.

UNIT 7 Food and drink

Ordering a meal in a restaurant

Vocabulario básico

el menú del día	the set menu
el gazpacho	the cold soup
la crema de espárragos	the asparagus soup
la ensalada mixta	the mixed salad
la tortilla española	the Spanish omelette
el pollo asado	the roast chicken
la chuleta de cerdo	the pork chop
la fritura de pescado	the fried fish
el pan	the bread
el postre	the dessert
después	after, next (*when ordering a meal*)
¿para beber?	what to drink?
el vino	the wine
blanco	white
tinto	red (*of wine*)
de la casa	house wine
el helado	the ice cream

Diálogo

Camarero	Buenas tardes, señora. ¿Qué va a tomar?
Clienta	Tráigame una ensalada mixta.
Camarero	¿Y después?
Clienta	Voy a tomar el pollo asado.
Camarero	¿Con patatas?
Clienta	Sí, con patatas.
Camarero	Y, ¿para beber? ¿Toma vino?
Clienta	Sí. Una botella de vino tinto de la casa.
Camarero	En seguida, señora.
	(*Más tarde*)
Camarero	¿Toma postre, señora?
Clienta	Sí, un helado de chocolate.

Ejercicios

1 Look at the following notes from a waiter's pad, and decide which dishes have been ordered from the menu.

1. C. de esp.
2. Ens. m.
3. Tor. esp.
4. Chul. de c.
5. Vi. bl.

2 On the recording two people are ordering meals from the **Menú del día**. Fill in the grid to show what each one orders.

First course	Second course	Drinks
1.		
2.		

3 Recreate the dialogue on the facing page, using the visual cues to help you. (*Answers on page 127.*)

Lenguaje

Just as **póngame** (+ noun) will enable you to get drinks and snacks in a café, fruit etc. in a market, and petrol in a petrol station, so *tráigame*, 'bring me', will enable you to order a meal adequately.

Tráigame el menú	Bring me the menu.
Tráigame una ensalada mixta.	Bring me a mixed salad.
Tráigame la cuenta.	Bring me the bill.

Ir + **a** + verb allows you to say what you are going to do.

Voy a tomar una tortilla española.	I'm going to have a Spanish omelette.
Juan va a visitar Toledo.	John is going to visit Toledo.

La vida española

Restaurants in Spain are classified by forks, with five forks given to the highest-class restaurants down to one fork for the cheapest. A restaurant with three forks is usually acceptable, but you can decide whether any restaurant is what you want, because nearly all of them display their full menu with prices in the window, and you can check before you go in. The **Menú del día** or the **Menú turístico** is usually the cheapest way to get a three-course meal.

UNIT 18

Travel

Obtaining information in the station

Vocabulario básico

va	goes, is going
no lo sé	I do not know
pregunte	ask (*order*)
el revisor	the ticket-collector
ahí	there
viene	he/she comes
el departamento	the compartment
¿a qué hora llega?	at what time does it arrive?
¿conoce usted?	do you know?
barato	cheap
enfrente de	opposite

Diálogos

En la estación

Turista ¿Es éste el tren para Ciudad Real?
Viajero No, señorita. Este tren va a Toledo.
Turista Entonces, ¿de dónde sale el tren para Ciudad Real?
Viajero No lo sé, señorita. Pregunte al revisor. Ahí viene.

En el andén

Turista Perdón, señor. ¿De dónde sale el tren para Ciudad Real?
Revisor Andén número tres, señorita.
Turista Gracias.

En el departamento

Revisor Billetes, por favor.
Turista Aquí tiene usted. ¿A qué hora llega el tren a Ciudad Real?
Revisor Llega a las cinco y media, señorita.
Turista ¿Conoce usted un hotel barato en Ciudad Real?
Revisor El Hotel Castilla es bastante barato, y está enfrente de la estación.

Ejercicios

1 Reconstruct these sentences to do with travel by train, using the first letter of each word to help you. Each full stop represents a further letter.

(a) ¿A q. . h. . . s. . . e. p. . . . . . t. . . p. . . M. . . . . ?

(b) U. b. . . . . . d. i. . y v. . . . .

(c) ¿D. d. . . . s. . . e. t. . . ?

2 On the recording three people are enquiring about trains. Mark the following statements TRUE or FALSE.

Dialogue 1

1. The man is looking for the Valencia train. ______________
2. He is mistaken about the train he has chosen. ______________
3. The train leaves at 11.30 a.m. ______________

Dialogue 2

1. The woman thinks the train goes to Madrid. ______________
2. In fact, it is going to Seville. ______________
3. The train she wants is on platform 8. ______________

Dialogue 3

1. The woman wants to know when the train arrives in Toledo. ______________
2. She is looking for a first class hotel in Toledo. ______________
3. The ticket collector cannot advise her because he is not from Toledo. ______________

3 Recreate the dialogues on the facing page, using the appropriate verbal cues to help you. (*Answers on pages 127–8.*)

En la estación

- Ask if this is the train for Valencia.
- Say: 'Then where does the train for Valencia leave from?'

En el andén

- Ask the ticket-collector where the train for Valencia goes from?
- Thank him.

En el departamento

- Show him your ticket and ask him when the train will arrive in Valencia.
- Ask him if he knows a good hotel in Valencia.

Lenguaje

There are two verbs to express 'to know' in Spanish: **saber** and **conocer**.

Saber expresses 'to know' of *facts*. The 1st person singular is **sé** (marked with a stress mark to distinguish it from **se** as in **se llama Paco**). For example:

Sé el número de teléfono. I know the telephone number.

Conocer expresses 'to know' ('to be familiar with') of people and places. The 1st person singular is **conozco**. For example:

Conozco a su padre. I know your father.
Conozco Nueva York. I know New York.

La vida española

Train services in Spain can be fairly infrequent, and there is often only one train a day on many routes. It is advisable, therefore, to book seats some days before you intend to travel. To do this you go to a Renfe office (**Oficina de viajes RENFE**), to a travel agent (**Agencia de viajes**) or to the special ticket office at the station (**Venta anticipada**).

Free time

How the weather affects your leisure activities

Vocabulario básico

cuando	when
tomo el sol	I sunbathe
el jardín	the garden
o	or
la piscina	the swimming pool
la playa	the beach
el teatro	the theatre
me quedo en casa	I stay at home
escucho	I listen to
un disco	a record
veo la televisión	I watch television

Diálogo

Mujer	¿Qué hace usted cuando hace buen tiempo?
Hombre	Pues, tomo el sol en el jardín, o voy a la piscina.
Mujer	Y, ¿si hace mal tiempo?
Hombre	Entonces, me quedo en casa y escucho un disco. ¿Qué hace usted cuando hace mucho sol?
Mujer	Tomo el sol en la playa.
Hombre	Y, ¿si hace mucho frío?
Mujer	Voy al cine o al teatro, o veo la televisión.

Ejercicios

1 Follow the lines from the weather symbol to the activity and say what you do.

For example:  play tennis.

Cuando hace buen tiempo, practico el tenis.

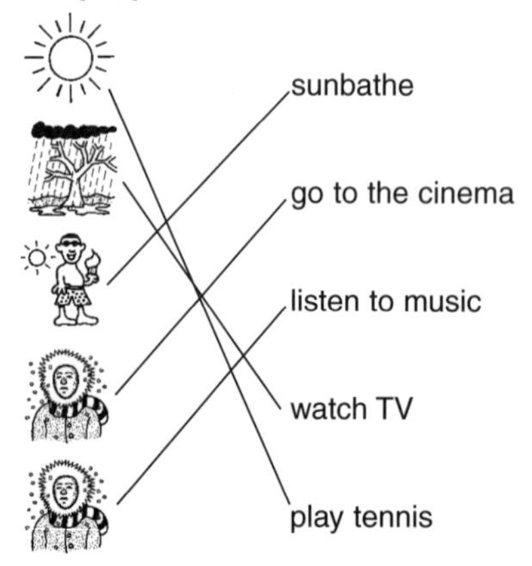

2 On the recording pairs of people are telling you what they do, given certain weather conditions. Fill in the grid below accordingly.

Weather conditions	Activities
1.	
2.	
3.	

3 Match up phrases from Column A with Column B to make sensible sentences.

A	B
Cuando hace buen tiempo ...	veo la televisión.
Si hace mucho frío ...	voy a la piscina.
Cuando hace mal tiempo ...	tomo el sol.
Si hace mucho sol ...	me quedo en casa.

Lenguaje

The verb **tomar** has now been used in three different ways.

Tome la segunda calle a la derecha. Take the second street on the right.

The verb **hacer**, 'to do', 'make', has an irregular 1st person singular.

¿Qué hace usted por la mañana? Hago café. What do you make in the morning? I make coffee.

La vida española

To find out what entertainments are available in Spain, look for the **Guía de espectáculos** (Entertainments Guide) in the local paper. In the same paper you can find the local weather forecast – **El tiempo**, or **Boletín meteorológico**. In large cities, **La guía del ocio** (Leisure Guide), available from newspaper kiosks, will list all the entertainments available.

Travel

Hiring a car

Vocabulario básico

alquilar	to hire
económico/a	economical
más	more, plus
por día	per day
queremos	we want, wish
visitar	to visit
el castillo	the castle
el kilómetro	the kilometre
listo	ready (*Note: used with* **estar**)
dentro de	within

Diálogo

En la agencia

Mujer	Buenos días. Aquí puedo alquilar un coche, ¿verdad?
Empleado	Eso es, señora. ¿Qué clase de coche quiere usted?
Mujer	Un coche económico.
Empleado	El Fiat Uno es muy económico, señora. Sólo vale cinco mil pesetas por día, más cuarenta pesetas por kilómetro.
Mujer	Un Fiat Uno, entonces.
Empleado	¿Para cuántos días?
Mujer	Para tres días. Queremos visitar el castillo de Peñafiel.
Empleado	Muy bien, señora. El coche va a estar listo dentro de diez minutos.

Ejercicios

1 Link the car name to the hire price per day by following the lines, and say aloud what each car costs. For example: **El Fiat Uno vale cinco mil pesetas por día.**

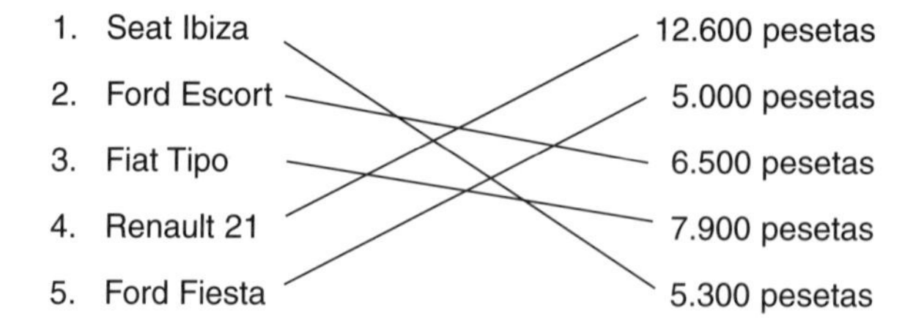

2 On the recording two people are hiring a car. Fill in the grid opposite according to what they say.

Type of car	Cost per day	Number of days
1.		
2.		

3 Recreate the dialogue on the facing page, using the cues to help you. (*Answers on page 128.*)

- Say good morning, and ask if you can hire a car here.
- Say you want an economical car.
- A Renault 5, then.
- You want it for two days. You want to visit El Escorial.

Lenguaje

To express 'we' (the 1st person plural) in Spanish, you make the verb end in **-mos**.

trabajar	to work
Trabajamos mucho.	We work a lot.

Irregular verbs also end **-mos** but the stem is different.

ser	to be
Somos ingleses.	We are English.

ir	to go
Vamos a visitar el castillo.	We are going to visit the castle.

'Per' is rendered in Spanish by **por**.

Cinco mil pesetas por día.	5.000 pesetas per day.
Mil pesetas por persona.	1.000 pesetas per person.

La vida española

Many hire car firms in Spain offer three tariffs: **Tarifa standard** is a daily charge plus a charge per kilometre travelled; **Kilometraje ilimitado** is a daily charge with unlimited mileage allows, and **Tarifa Business** is also a daily charge with unlimited mileage. It is often possible to achieve considerable reductions on car hire for Spain by booking through the London office of one of the international firms.

UNIT 2

Free time

A visit to Peñafiel

Vocabulario básico

pensar	to think
¿qué piensa usted hacer?	what are you thinking of doing?
el fin de semana	the weekend
ir a + verb	to be going to
vamos a visitar	we are going to visit
la provincia	the province
el siglo	the century
el público	the public
creo que sí/no	I think so/not
caro/a	dear, expensive
la entrada	the entrance ticket (*theatre*, *cinema*, *monuments*)
la guía	the guide book
decir	to say, tell (*Note:* **digo** = *I say, tell*)

Diálogo

Hombre	¿Qué piensa usted hacer este fin de semana?
Mujer	Mi marido y yo vamos a visitar Peñafiel.
Hombre	¿Dónde está Peñafiel?
Mujer	Está en la región de Castilla-León, cerca de Valladolid.
Hombre	Y, ¿qué hay de interés en Peñafiel?
Mujer	Hay un castillo del siglo catorce.
Hombre	¿Está abierto al público?
Mujer	Sí, creo que sí.
Hombre	¿Es cara la entrada?
Mujer	No. La guía dice que la entrada sólo vale cien pesetas.
Hombre	¡Qué bien!

Ejercicios

1 Match the Spanish words for buildings to the English words, writing down the number of the Spanish word, and the letter of the English.

1. La catedral	(a) The swimming pool	________	________
2. El banco	(b) The cafe	________	________
3. El castillo	(c) The house	________	________
4. La estación	(d) The cathedral	________	________
5. La plaza	(e) The cinema	________	________
6. El café	(f) The museum	________	________
7. La casa	(g) The bank	________	________
8. La piscina	(h) The castle	________	________
9. El museo	(i) The square	________	________
10. El cine	(j) The station	________	________

2 On the recording two people are outlining their plans for the weekend. Fill in the grid below to show which town they intend to visit and what they will see there.

Town visited	Place visited
1.	
2.	

3 Fill in the gaps to ask questions about a Spanish castle. (Each full stop = one letter).

¿ Dónde está el c . . . .? ¿ Qué hay de i. . . . . . para los turistas?

¿ Está a . . . . . . al público? ¿ Es c . . . la entrada?

Lenguaje

A verb in Spanish can be divided into two parts: the ending **-ar**, **-er**, **-ir**, and the stem, which is the first part. Some verbs, known as stem-changing verbs, change the stem as follows:

o or **u** to **ue**		**e** to **ie**	
Poder, 'to be able, can'		**Pensar**, 'to think'	
puedo	I can	**pienso**	I think
puedes	you can	**piensas**	you think
puede	he/she can	**piensa**	he/she thinks
usted puede	you can	**usted piensa**	you think

La vida española

The Moors invaded Spain in AD 711, conquered virtually the whole of Spain, and were finally expelled in 1492. As the operation to expel them – **La Reconquista** – proceeded south, lines of castles were built across the country to protect the reconquered lands. Many of these castles, such as Peñafiel, still exist, and many have been converted into luxury hotels – **Paradores** – which are well worth a visit.

UNIT 22 Emergencies

At the chemist's

Vocabulario básico

la farmacia	the chemist's
el farmacéutico	the chemist
el dolor	the pain, ache
el estómago	the stomach
el paquete	the packet
la cabeza	the head
las quemaduras del sol	sunburn
el tubo	the tube
excelente	excellent
el comprimido	the tablet
la garganta	the throat
la muela	the tooth (molar)
la diarrea	the diarrhoea

Diálogo

Turista	Buenos días. ¿Tiene algo para el dolor de estómago?
Farmacéutico	Sí, señora. OKAL es muy bueno. Quinientas pesetas el paquete. ¿Algo más?
Turista	Sí. Algo para el dolor de cabeza.
Farmacéutico	Esto es muy bueno. Doscientas pesetas el paquete. ¿Eso es todo?
Turista	No. ¿Qué tiene para las quemaduras del sol?
Farmacéutico	Esta crema es excelente. Setecientas pesetas el tubo.
Turista	¿Cuánto es todo?
Farmacéutico	Son mil cuatrocientas pesetas, señora.

Ejercicios

1 What would you say to the chemist to get medicine for the following conditions?

2 On the recording three people are asking for medicines in the chemist's. Mark the following sentences TRUE or FALSE, and try to correct the false ones.

1. She has sunburn and is given a tube of cream for 500 pesetas. ________
2. He has a headache and is given some tablets, which cost 300 pesetas. ________
3. The girl has a stomach-ache and is given OKAL, which costs 550 pesetas. ________

3 What do you say to the chemist to ask the following questions:

(a) Do you have something for a headache?
(b) Do you have something for sunburn?
(c) Give me a tube, please.
(d) How much is all that?

Lenguaje

To express a pain or an ache in Spanish you use the phrase **el dolor de** + the part of the body concerned. Thus:

el dolor de estómago	stomach-ache
el dolor de cabeza	headache
el dolor de garganta	sore throat
el dolor de muelas	toothache

To ask for medicine in a chemist's, you use the phrase: **¿tiene algo para** + the problem.

¿Tiene algo para el dolor de garganta?	Do you have something for a sore throat?

La vida española

Many Spaniards go first to the chemist when they feel ill, and not to the doctor. This means the chemists in Spain are skilled at diagnosing and treating many common problems encountered by tourists, such as stomach-ache, sunburn etc. Medicines in Spain tend to be rather expensive and many more medicines are available without prescription than in some other countries.

My family and I

Talking about your family

Vocabulario básico

los hermanos	the brothers and sisters
el hermano	the brother
la hermana	the sister
¿Cómo es/son?	What is he/she like? What are they like?
alto/a	tall
bajo/a	short, small
gordo/a	fat
delgado/a	thin
el pelo	the hair
largo/a	long
corto/a	short
moreno	dark (*hair*), brown
rubio	fair (*hair*)
el ojo	the eye
negro/a	black
gris	grey
guapo/a	pretty, handsome
inteligente	clever
único/a	only (*child*), unique

Diálogo

Paco ¿Tiene usted hermanos, doña Isabel?
Isabel Sí, tengo dos: un hermano y una hermana.
Paco ¿Cómo son?
Isabel Pues, mi hermana Ana es bastante alta y delgada. Tiene el pelo moreno muy largo y los ojos negros.
Paco Y ¿tu hermano?
Isabel Juan es bajo y bastante gordo. Tiene el pelo corto y rubio y los ojos grises.
Paco ¿Es guapa Ana?
Isabel Sí, es muy guapa. También es muy inteligente. ¿Tiene usted hermanos?
Paco No. Soy hijo único.

1. 
2. 
3. 
4. 

Ejercicios

1 Match the description to the pictures on the previous page.

(a) Es baja y gorda. Tiene el pelo corto. (b) Es alto y delgado. Tiene el pelo muy largo. (c) Es bajo y delgado. Tiene el pelo largo. (d) Es alta y guapa. Tiene el pelo corto.

2 Make as many sentences as you can, taking one element from each column.

	padre		25		alto
Mi	hermano	tiene	39	años. Es	bajo
	hijo		40		gordo
					delgado

	madre		27		alta
Mi	hermana	tiene	56	años. Es	baja
	hija		35		delgada.

3 Recreate the dialogue on the facing page, using the written cues to help you. (*Answers on page 128.*)

- Say 'Yes, I have two: a brother and a sister.'
- Your sister is tall and slim. She has very long hair.
- He is short and fat. He has short hair.
- Yes, she is very intelligent.

Lenguaje

To change the meaning of an adjective slightly, you use one of the following:

Es barato.	It's cheap.
Es <u>bastante</u> barato.	It's fairly cheap.
Es <u>muy</u> barato.	It's very cheap.

English has 'It's very, very cheap', but Spanish has a further form. This is made by adding **-ísimo** to the end of the adjective.

Este hotel es baratísimo. This hotel is very, very cheap.

La vida española

When you know people well in Spain, **don** and **doña** are no longer used, and you simply use their first names. **Buenos días, Isabel. Hola, Paco.** You also use the 2nd person singular of the verb when you speak to them. **Buenos días, Isabel. ¿Cómo estás? Hola, Paco. ¿Adónde vas?** 'Good morning Isabel. How are you? Hello, Paco. Where are you going?'

Travel

Finding your way by car

Vocabulario básico

la carretera	the road
¿qué tengo que hacer?	what do I have to do?
para (+ infinitive)	in order to (do something)
volver	to return
coger	to take (*of road*), catch (*bus, train, cold, etc.*)
¿cuánto se tarda en llegar?	how long does it take to arrive?
está a (number) **kilómetros**	it's (number) kilometres
unos (+ number)	about (+ number)

Diálogo

Turista Perdón, señor. ¿Es ésta la carretera para Ciudad Real?
Transeúnte No, señora. Esta carretera va a Valencia.
Turista ¿Qué tengo que hacer para llegar a Ciudad Real?
Transeúnte Tiene usted que volver al pueblo y coger la carretera número cuatrocientos veinte. Esa carretera va a Ciudad Real.
Turista Y, ¿cuánto se tarda en llegar a Ciudad Real?
Transeúnte Pues, está a unos ciento veinte kilómetros de aquí. Se tarda dos horas en llegar.
Turista Gracias, señor.

Ejercicios

1

	TOLEDO	VALENCIA	VALLADOLID	VITORIA	ZAMORA
VALENCIA	372				
VALLADOLID	258	545			
VITORIA	422	576	236		
ZAMORA	296	600	96	332	
ZARAGOZA	396	326	367	258	463

Answer the following questions:

For example: ¿A qué distancia está Valencia de Zaragoza? Está a trescientos veintiséis kilómetros.

1. ¿A qué distancia está Toledo de Vitoria?
2. ¿Y Valencia de Zamora?
3. ¿Y Toledo de Valladolid?
4. ¿Y Zamora de Valladolid?

Cross reference with units: 7 18 20

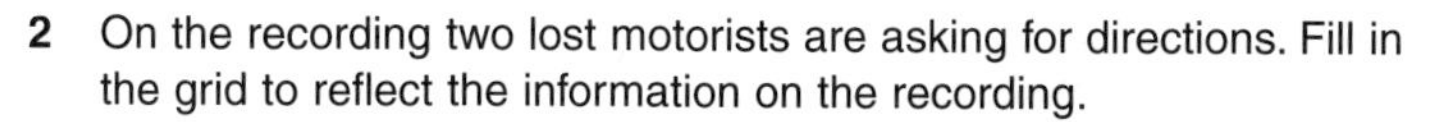

2 On the recording two lost motorists are asking for directions. Fill in the grid to reflect the information on the recording.

Driver's destination	Road number to take	Journey time
1.		
2.		

3 Recreate the dialogue on the facing page, using the verbal cues to help you. (*Answers on page 128.*)

- Say 'Excuse me, is this the road for Toledo?'
- Ask what you have to do to get to Toledo.
- Ask how long it will take to get there.
- Thank him.

Lenguaje

Saying that you have to do something is expressed by using the verb **tener** + **que** + infinitive.

Tengo que volver a Ciudad Real. I have to return to Ciudad Real.

Coger is vulgar in Latin American Spanish, and you should use the verb tomar.

Tome la primera a la derecha. Take the first on the right.

To express how much time you take to do something, you use **tardar en** (+ an expression of time).

¿Cuánto tiempo se tarda en llegar?	How long does it take to arrive?
Se tarda dos horas.	It takes two hours.

La vida española

Most roads in Spain tend not to be very crowded. Petrol stations are not widely found, and it is best to fill up when the petrol gauge falls below half. Motorways (**Autopistas**) are marked on Spanish road maps by parallel blue lines; dual carriageways (**Autovías**) are marked by parallel red lines; 'A' roads (**N** for **Nacional**) are indicated by a single red line and 'B' roads (**C** for **Comarcal**) are shown by a green line.

In the hotel

Booking a hotel room by telephone

Vocabulario básico

el teléfono	the telephone
dígame	hello (*on the telephone. Literally:* tell me)
oiga	hello (*on the telephone*)
la noche	the night
el momento	the moment
lo siento	I'm sorry
completo	full (*of hotel*)
no ... nada	nothing
¡qué lástima!	what a pity
otro	another

Diálogo

Recepcionista	Buenas tardes. Hotel Pintor. Dígame.
Hombre	Buenas tardes. ¿Tiene una habitación libre?
Recepcionista	¿Para qué día, señor?
Hombre	Para hoy.
Recepcionista	Un momento, por favor, señor. Oiga. Lo siento pero el hotel está completo. No tengo nada libre para hoy ...
Hombre	¡Qué lástima! ¿Conoce usted otro hotel en Toledo?
Recepcionista	El Hotel Almazara es muy bueno, señor.
Hombre	¿Tiene el número de teléfono de ese hotel?
Recepcionista	Sí. El número de teléfono es veintidós, treinta y ocho, sesenta y seis.
Hombre	Muchas gracias.

Ejercicios

1 Look at the picture and write down all the names of things which contain the letter **a** in Spanish.

Cross reference with units:

2 On the recording two travellers are trying to book a hotel room. Mark the following statements TRUE or FALSE and correct what is false.

1. The hotel is full, but the Hotel Los Tilos, phone 31 80 89 is recommended. __________

2. The hotel is able to offer a room for tonight at 6,000 pesetas. __________

3 ¿Qué se dice? (What does one say?)

Express in Spanish.

a) Have you a room free?

b) For today.

c) I'm sorry.

d) I have nothing free.

e) Do you have the telephone number for that hotel.

f) Thank you very much.

Lenguaje

To express 'nothing' in Spanish, the key word is **nada**, which is placed after the verb, with **no** in front:

No tengo nada libre. I have nothing free.

Regret is expressed with the phrase: **Lo siento**, 'I'm sorry'.

La vida española

In Spanish, telephone numbers are usually given in pairs: 22 38 66 = **veintidós**, **treinta y ocho**, **sesenta y seis**. When answering your phone you say: **Dígame**, and the caller says: **Oiga**. If you are asked to identify yourself, the telephonist will normally say: **¿De parte de quién?** and you give a simple identification: **Soy el señor/la señora/la señorita** + your surname.

Goods and services

Obtaining information in a Tourist Office

Vocabulario básico

la oficina de turismo	the Tourist Office
el empleado	the employee
el plano	the plan
gratis	free (of charge)
la cosa	the thing
las murallas	the city walls
varios/as	several
el palacio	the palace
¿puede darme ... ?	can you give me ... ?
el mapa	the map
la ruta	the route
turístico/a	tourist (*adj.*)
adiós	goodbye

Diálogo

Turista Buenos días. ¿Tiene usted un plano de la ciudad?
Empleado Aquí tiene usted, señora.
Turista ¿Cuánto vale?
Empleado Nada, señora. Es gratis.
Turista Muchas gracias. ¿Qué hay para los turistas en Avila?
Empleado Muchas cosas. Primero, tiene usted las murallas. Luego hay la catedral, que es del siglo catorce, y muchos palacios antiguos.
Turista Gracias. ¿Puede darme también un mapa de la región?
Empleado Sí, señora. Y en el mapa puede ver varias rutas turísticas.
Turista Muchas gracias. Adiós.

Ejercicios

1 Match the captions to the pictures, writing down the number of the picture and the letter of the caption.

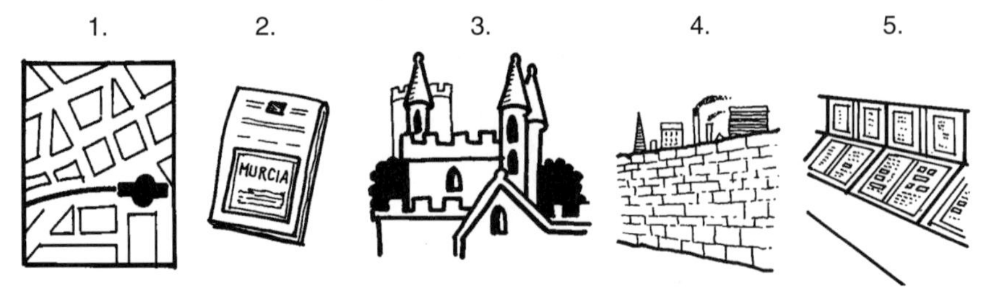

(a) El museo. (b) El castillo. (c) Un plano de la ciudad. (d) Las murallas. (e) Un mapa de la región.

________ ________ ________ ________ ________

Cross reference with units:

2 Reconstruct the following questions. Each full stop equals one letter.

a) ¿T . . . . u. p . . . . d. l. c . . . . .?
b) ¿C . . . . . v . . .?
c) ¿Q . . h . . p . . . l . . t . . . . e. A . . . .?

3 Recreate the dialogue on the facing page, using the verbal cues to help you. (*Answers on pages 128–9.*)

- Say good morning. Ask if he has a town plan.
- Ask how much it costs.
- Ask what there is for tourists in Sevilla.
- Ask if he can give you a map of the region.

Lenguaje

To make a polite request in Spanish, you use one of two forms + the infinitive of the second verb.

¿Puede usted darme . . . ?	Can you give me . . . ?
¿Quiere usted decirme . . . ?	Will you tell me . . . ?

The word for 'much' or 'many' is **mucho**, and agrees with the noun it precedes:

Hay muchas cosas para los turistas.	There are lots of things for tourists.
No tengo mucho dinero.	I don't have much money.

La vida española

Spain is very well provided with Tourist Offices; every town (and even village) will have one, and it will be clearly signposted. You can obtain information about the area, maps, guides and hotel lists with prices (**La lista de hoteles**). Before going to Spain, you can obtain all of this information material from the Spanish National Tourist Office at 57, St James Street, London SW1A 1LD.

Goods and services

Buying tourist souvenirs

Vocabulario básico

la tienda	the shop
el recuerdo	the souvenir, memory
típico/a	typical
la cerámica	the ceramics, pottery
se fabrica	it is made (*See* **Lenguaje**)
el plato	the plate
la jarra	the jug
no comprendo	I don't understand
rojo/a	red
más ... que	more ... than (*See* **Lenguaje**)
éste/a	this (one)
ése/a	that (one)

Diálogo

Turista	Buenos días. ¿Tiene algo típico de esta región?
Empleado	Sí, señora. La cerámica es típica de aquí.
Turista	Y, ¿se fabrica por aquí?
Empleado	Sí, señora, se fabrica en todos los pueblos.
Turista	¿Qué tiene usted exactamente?
Empleado	Pues, hay platos, jarras ...
Turista	Lo siento. No comprendo. ¿Qué es una jarra?
Empleado	Ahí tiene usted una. Es para el agua o el vino.
Turista	¡Ah sí! Ahora comprendo.
Empleado	Este plato rojo y blanco es muy bonito, ¿no?
Turista	Sí, pero, ¿tiene uno más pequeño?
Empleado	¿Este?
Turista	Sí, ése es muy bonito. ¿Cuánto vale?
Empleado	Setecientas pesetas, señora.
Turista	Muy bien. Ése, por favor.

Ejercicios

1 Follow the lines to work out how much each object costs. Say the price aloud.

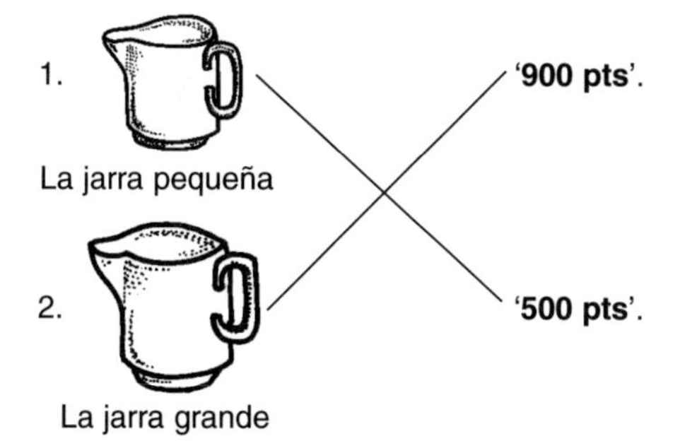

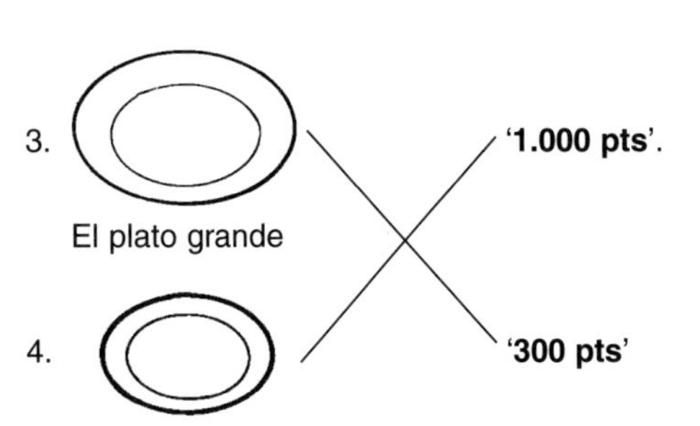

El plato pequeño

2 True or False? On the recording three people are buying pottery. Mark the following statements True or False, and check your answers on page 129.

1. She buys a yellow and white jug for 3.000 pesetas.
2. He asks to see a smaller blue and black plate and buys it for 4.000 pesetas.
3. She asks to see a bigger white jug and buys it for 1.500 pesetas.

3 Use the English cues, given in brackets, to help you complete the conversation about buying a jug.

a) (Say you are sorry but do not understand. What is 'una jarra'?)
Ahí tiene usted una. Es para el agua o el vino.
b) (Say yes, now you understand)
Esta jarra roja y blanca es muy bonita, ¿no?
c) (Say yes, but does he have a bigger one)
¿Esta?
d) (Say yes, and ask the price)
Novecientas pesetas.
e) (Say that one, please)

Lenguaje

To express 'is made' or 'are made' you use the 3rd person singular or plural of the verb **fabricar** + the pronoun **se**.

¿Dónde se fabrica la cerámica? Se fabrica en todos los pueblos.
Where is pottery made? It is made in all the villages.

¿Dónde se fabrican los coches? Se fabrican en Valencia.
Where are cars made? They are made in Valencia.

To compare one thing with another, you can use **más** ('more') before the adjective and **que** after it.

El vino es más caro que la cerveza. Wine is more expensive than beer.

La vida española

Tourist shops are common in Spain and usually stock goods produced by local craftsmen. Leather goods are usually good value, and ceramics are produced throughout the country, although Talavera de la Reina is probably the best centre. The cynical view that a tourist is 'someone who goes abroad and buys rubbish' should be heeded carefully!

Food and drink

Ordering a meal in a restaurant

Vocabulario básico

el melón	the melon
¿qué le apetece?	what do you fancy?
el bistec	the steak
bien hecho	well done
poco hecho	rare (*of meat*)
la fruta	the fruit
la manzana	the apple
la pera	the pear
el plátano	the banana
la fresa	the strawberry
el coñac	the brandy
la cuenta	the bill
tengo prisa	I'm in a hurry

Diálogo

Camarero	Buenos días, señora. ¿Qué va a tomar?
Clienta	¿Qué tal el melón?
Camarero	Está muy bueno, señora.
Clienta	El melón con jamón, entonces.
Camarero	Y, ¿de segundo plato? ¿Qué le apetece?
Clienta	Un bistec con patatas.
Camarero	¿Bien hecho o poco hecho?
Clienta	Bien hecho, por favor.
Camarero	Y, ¿para beber?
Clienta	Una botella de vino tinto.
	. . .
Camarero	¿Toma postre, señora?
Clienta	¿Qué fruta tiene?
Camarero	Pues, hay manzanas, peras, plátanos, fresas …
Clienta	Una pera, por favor. Y la cuenta. Tengo prisa.

Ejercicios

1 Fill in the missing vowels from the following, and then write down the English equivalents. (*Answers on page 129.*)

(a) . n b . st . c
(b) P . t . t . s fr . t . s
(c) . n . m . nz . n .
(d) . n . p . r .
(e) . n pl . t . n .
(f) fr . s . s

Cross reference with units:

6

17

2 On the recording three people are ordering things in a restaurant. Select the correct meal for each customer from the lists below.

1. (a) Mixed salad; rare steak with chips; bottle of house white wine.
   (b) Mixed salad; well-done steak; bottle of red wine.
   (c) Fish soup; rare steak with salad; bottle of mineral water.
2. (a) Ice-cream. (b) Cheese. (c) Strawberries.
3. (a) A black coffee. (b) A black coffee and a brandy. (c) A white coffee.

3 Recreate the dialogue on the facing page, using the visual cues to help you.

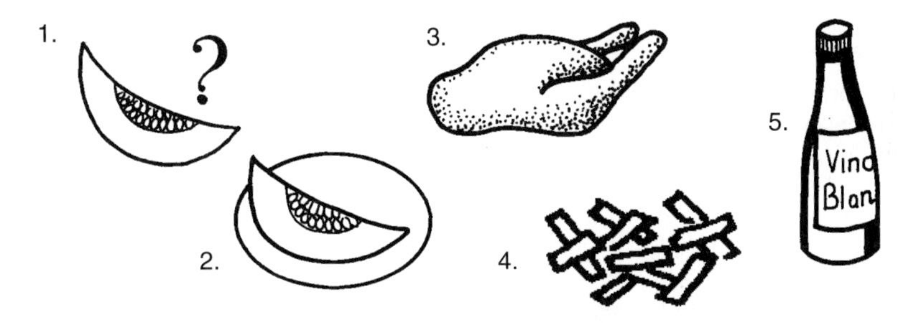

Lenguaje

¿Qué tal (+ noun)**?** enables you to ask how something is.

¿Qué tal el hotel?	What's the hotel like?

Apetecer, 'to fancy', is used to express what you fancy having.

Me apetece un bistec bien hecho.	I fancy a well-done steak.

Tener prisa is used to express being in a hurry.

Tengo prisa.	I'm in a hurry.

La vida española

In Spain, 3-fork restaurants and above usually have an English version of the menu.

Spanish chefs think that the English cremate meat. Therefore **bien hecho** will mean to English tastes that the meat is 'medium'.

By law restaurants and bars must have a **Libro de reclamaciones** (Complaints Book). Ask for it if you are very disappointed by the standards.

Travel

Travel by taxi

Vocabulario básico

la parada (**de taxis**)	the stop (*bus*), rank (*taxis*)
¿adónde?	to where?
llevar	to take (*people*), wear (*clothes*)
la	you (*feminine pronoun*)
el aeropuerto	the airport
el vuelo	the flight
la salida	the departure (*travel*), exit (*building*)
la llegada	the arrival
nacional	national
internacional	international
encantador/a	charming
¿Qué le debo?	What do I owe you?
el viaje	the journey

Diálogos

En la parada de taxis

Viajera ¿Está libre?
Taxista Sí, señora. ¿Adónde la llevo?
Viajera Al aeropuerto, por favor.
Taxista ¿Tiene usted prisa?
Viajera No, no tengo prisa. El vuelo sale a las cinco.
Taxista Muy bien.

En el taxi

Taxista ¿Salidas o llegadas, señora?
Viajera Salidas, por favor.
Taxista ¿Nacionales o internacionales?
Viajera Nacionales, por favor.
Taxista ¿Adónde va usted, señora?
Viajera Voy a Sevilla. ¿Conoce usted Sevilla?
Taxista Sí, señora. Es una ciudad encantadora.

En el aeropuerto

Taxista Aquí estamos, señora. Salidas nacionales.
Viajera Gracias. ¿Qué le debo?
Taxista Son mil doscientas pesetas, señora.
Viajera Aquí tiene usted.
Taxista Gracias, señora, y muy buen viaje.

Cross reference with units: 7 18 20 24

Ejercicios

1 Follow the lines and discover where each traveller is going. Say aloud their destination. For example: **El señor Pérez va a Córdoba**.

1. El señor Pérez — Málaga
2. La señora González — Córdoba
3. La señorita Losada — Bilbao
4. El señor Amodia — Granada

2 On the recording three people are giving instructions to a taxi-driver. Fill in the grid to record the information they give.

Taxi destination	In a hurry or not
1.	
2.	
3.	

3 How do you answer the taxi driver's questions if:

a) You want the Departures section of the airport.
   – ¿Salidas o llegadás?
b) You want International departures.
   – ¿Nacionales o internacionales?
c) You are going to London.
   – ¿Adónde va usted?

Lenguaje

You have now seen three forms of the word for 'Where?' **¿Dónde?** is used for a fixed position: **¿Dónde está el bar?** 'Where is the bar?' **¿De dónde?** is used to ask for origins: **¿De dónde es usted?** 'Where are you from?' and **¿Adónde?** is used to ask about destinations: **¿Adónde va usted?** 'Where are you going to?'

The verb **deber** means 'must', 'to have to' or 'to owe'. The phrase **¿Qué le debo?** can be used to ask about the cost in bars, of taxi-drivers etc.

La vida española

Spanish taxis are easy to recognise because they usually have a coloured stripe around the car. If a taxi is free, it displays the **Libre** sign, and if it is occupied, **Ocupado**. At night these signs are replaced by a green or red light. Taxis sometimes serve as emergency ambulances. When they are performing this service, the driver sounds his horn continuously and waves a white handkerchief out of the window.

UNIT 30

Free time

Likes and dislikes

Vocabulario básico

me	me (*pronoun*)
le	you (*masculine and feminine pronoun to replace* **usted**)
gustar	to please (to like) (*See* **Lenguaje**, *below*)
aburrido	boring
divertido	amusing
nadar	to swim
la amiga	the friend (*female*)
¿cuál?	which?
el pasatiempo	the pastime
bien	well
jugar	to play (games)

Diálogo

Hombre ¿Le gusta el fútbol?
Mujer No, no me gusta. Es muy aburrido.
Hombre ¿Qué le gusta, entonces?
Mujer Me gusta mucho el golf. Juego al golf los martes.
Hombre ¿Juega usted al golf con su marido?
Mujer No, con mi amiga Dolores.
Hombre ¡Qué interesante!
Mujer ¿Cuál es su pasatiempo favorito?
Hombre Me gusta mucho nadar. Voy a la piscina el viernes con mi hijo.
Mujer Y, ¿nada usted bien?
Hombre Sí, nado bastante bien.
Mujer ¡Qué divertido!

Ejercicios

1 Sort out these scrambled sentences.

(a) al tenis juego jardín en el.
(b) ¿deporte practica algún?
(c) a aficionado novelas soy las.
(d) ¿su libre hace usted qué en tiempo?

2 On the recording people are explaining what they do in their free time. Fill in the grid to show what they do, where, and with whom.

Activity	Place	With whom
1.		
2.		
3.		

Cross reference with units: 8 19 21

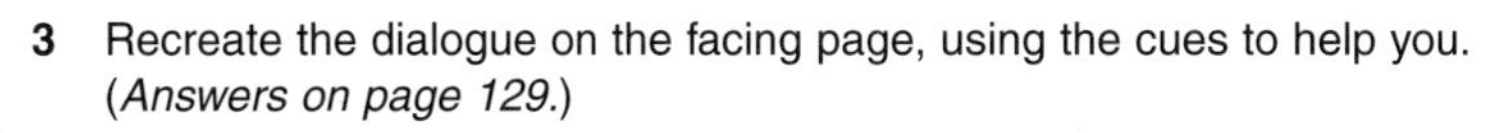

3 Recreate the dialogue on the facing page, using the cues to help you. (*Answers on page 129.*)

- Say you don't like it. It's very boring.
- You like tennis a lot.
- You play it with your friend Lola.
- Ask what is his favourite pastime.

Lenguaje

To express 'likes and dislikes' you use the verb **gustar**, which means 'to please'. The English sentence becomes transformed as follows:

I like beer – Beer pleases me – **Me gusta el vino.**
I like to swim – Swimming pleases me – **Me gusta nadar.**

A sentence expressing dislike follows a similar pattern.

I don't like tennis – Tennis doesn't please me – **No me gusta el tenis.**
I don't like playing golf – Playing golf doesn't please me – **No me gusta jugar al golf.**

Other persons – he, she, you (**usted**) – are all expressed using the pronoun **le**.

¿Le gusta el tenis? Do you like tennis?

La vida española

To find out what leisure activities are available in large cities, you consult the **Ocio, Deporte** (Leisure, Sport) in the **Guía del ocio** (Leisure Guide). In daily newspapers the section **Deportes** (Sports) will report on sporting events in the area.

UNIT 3 The weather

Talking about how weather affects what you do

Vocabulario básico

te	you (2nd person pronoun) (*See* **Lenguaje**)
dar	to give (*Note:* **doy**, 'I give'. *See* **Lenguaje**)
dar un paseo	to go for a walk
por el campo	in the countryside
llueve	it rains
nieva	it snows
el salón	the sitting-room
leer	to read
esquiar	to ski
la sierra	the mountains
me gusta más	I prefer (it pleases me more) (*See* **Lenguaje**)
me gustan más	I prefer (they please me more) (*See* **Lenguaje**)

Diálogo

Hombre ¿Qué te gusta hacer cuando hace sol, María?
María Me gusta dar un paseo por el campo.
Hombre Y, ¿cuando llueve y no puedes salir?
María Me gusta leer un libro en el salón.
Hombre ¿Qué clase de libros te gusta más?
María Me gustan más las novelas románticas.
Hombre ¡Qué interesante!
María ¿Qué te gusta hacer cuando hace calor?
Hombre Me gusta ir a la playa con la familia.
María Y cuando nieva, ¿qué te gusta hacer?
Hombre Me gusta esquiar en la sierra.

Ejercicios

1 Follow the lines to find out which thing or activity each person prefers. Say aloud what each one prefers. For example, Marta says: **Me gusta más el pescado.**

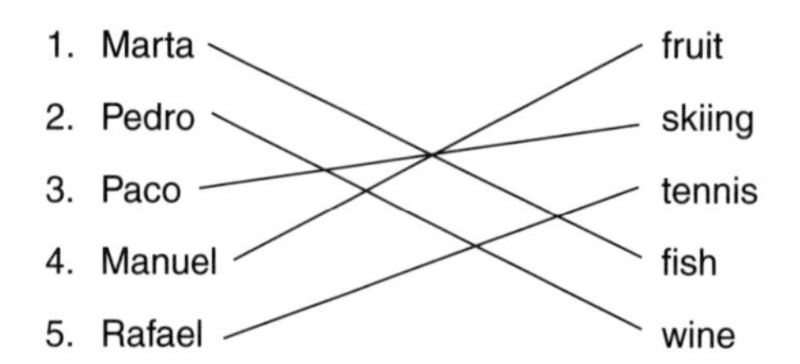

2 Sense or Nonsense? Do these sentences make sense or nonsense?

(a) Cuando hace sol me gusta esquiar por la ciudad.
(b) Cuando llueve me gusta ver la televisión.
(c) Cuando llueve me gusta leer un libro en la sierra.
(d) Cuando nieva me gusta ir a la playa.

3 Recreate the dialogue on the facing page, using the cues below to help you. (*Answers on page 129.*)
You like doing the following:

- Walking in the countryside.
- Watching television.
- Watching sports programmes on the television.

Lenguaje

When talking to members of your family, friends, children or animals, you address them in the 2nd person of the verb, without a pronoun (here, the word for 'you'). The verb *always* ends in **-s**.

Comprendes el español.	You understand Spanish.
Hablas muy bien el español.	You speak Spanish very well.

The pronoun used with **gustar** is **te**.

¿Te gusta el vino?	Do you like wine?

If what you like or prefer is plural, the verb changes to **gustan**.

Me gustan más las novelas románticas.	I prefer romantic novels.

La vida española

The guaranteed summer sunshine has made Spain the favourite holiday destination of British tourists, and they flock in their millions to the many 'Costas' found on the northern, mediterranean and southern coasts.

Families with young children might prefer to visit the Costa Verde on the northern coast where the summer weather is similar to a good British summer.

My family and I

Talking about your daily routine

Vocabulario básico

la vida	the life
diario/a	daily
el ama de casa	the housewife
la mañana	the morning
me levanto	I get up
levantarse	to get up
luego	then, next
me visto	I get dressed
vestirse	to get dressed
el trabajo	the work, job
imposible	impossible
aparcar	to park (*a car*)
el autobús	the bus
empiezo	I begin
empezar	to begin
terminar	to end
sobre	at about (*of time*)

Diálogo

Pedro	¿Trabajas o eres ama de casa?
Marta	Trabajo, pero sólo por la mañana.
Pedro	¿Cómo es tu vida diaria, entonces?
Marta	Pues me levanto a las seis.
Pedro	¿Y luego?
Marta	Me visto y tomo el desayuno.
Pedro	¿Cómo vas al trabajo? ¿En coche?
Marta	No. Es imposible aparcar en la ciudad.
Pedro	¿Vas a pie?
Marta	No. Cojo el autobús.
Pedro	¿A qué hora empiezas el trabajo?
Marta	A las ocho y media, y termino a eso de la una.

Ejercicios

1 Say when each person begins and ends work. For example:

	8:00	**Manuel**	**6:00**

Manuel empieza a las ocho y termina a las seis.

1.	**9:00**	María	**5:00**
2.	**10:00**	Pedro	**7:00**
3.	**12:00**	Juan	**10:00**
4.	**3:00**	Lola	**7:00**

2 These are the answers, but, what were the questions?

(a) Me levanto a las ocho.
(b) Empiezo mi trabajo a las nueve.
(c) El trabajo es bastante aburrido.
(d) Termino a las seis de la tarde.

3 Recreate the dialogue on the facing page, using the visual cues to help you. (*Answers on page 129.*)

Cross reference with units: 1 12 23

Lenguaje

The verb **empezar**, 'to begin', changes when using the present tense as follows:

empiezo	I begin
empiezas	you begin
empieza	he/she/it begins

Vestirse, 'to get dressed', changes the **e** to **i** in the same persons.

me visto	I get dressed
te vistes	you get dressed
se viste	he/she/it gets dressed

La vida española

The myth of the idle Spaniard is all part of the **Leyenda negra** (Black Legend), and most Spaniards are extremely hard-working. In fact, many work a **jornada intensiva**, which is an eight-hour working day with little or no rest. Having completed the **jornada intensiva**, they may go on to another job, and work many more hours.

UNIT 33

Making plans

Arranging to meet

Vocabulario básico

creo que sí/no	I think so/not
¿por qué?	why?
porque	because
jugar	to play (*games*)
el partido	the game, match
la idea	the idea
verse	to meet, to see each other
delante de	in front of
quedar	to agree (*a time*), to remain, to have left over
tu, tus	your (*speaking to a friend*)
¿vale?	O.K.?

Diálogo

Juan ¡Hola, María! ¿Estás libre el sábado por la tarde?
María Sí, creo que sí. ¿Por qué me preguntas?
Juan Porque quiero jugar un partido de golf. ¿Te apetece?
María ¡Qué buena idea!
Juan ¿Dónde nos vemos?
María Delante de tu casa.
Juan Muy bien. ¿A qué hora quedamos?
María A las tres de la tarde. ¿Vale?
Juan Vale. Hasta el sábado.
María Adiós. Hasta el sábado.

Ejercicios

1 Produce a sentence to invite a friend to go to the following places. For example:

¿Por qué no vamos al teatro?

1. 

2. 

3. 

4. 

2 On the recording two couples are arranging to meet. Fill in the grid to indicate where they will meet, for what reason, where, and at what time.

Day of week	Reason	Place	Time
1.			
2.			

3 Recreate the dialogue on the facing page, using the verbal cues to help you. (*Answers on page 129.*)

- Say yes, you think so.
- What 'What a good idea.'
- Say 'In front of the Café Sol.'
- Say 'At 2 p.m. Is that OK?

Lenguaje

¿Por qué ...? means 'Why ...?

¿Por qué me preguntas?	Why are you asking me?

Porque ... means 'Because ...'

Porque quiero saber.	Because I want to know.

Pronouns precede the verb usually in Spanish, and the pronoun for 'me', 'to me' or 'myself' is always **me**.

Me pregunta la hora.	He asks me the time.
Me da el sandwich.	He gives the sandwich to me.
Me llamo Roberto.	I call myself Robert. My name is Robert.

La vida española

Sport in Spain used to be largely spectator sports, with tens of thousands going to see famous football teams like Real Madrid. Now things have changed, and as a sportsman or woman becomes famous, the sport they play becomes fashionable. Severiano Ballesteros brought golf into prominence in the 1980s and nowadays Delgado, who has won the Tour de France twice, and Sánchez Vicario, who appears regularly at Wimbledon, have made cycling and tennis very popular.

My family and I

Talking about the family

Vocabulario básico

la foto	the photo
la familia	the family
la madre	the mother
el padre	the father
los padres	the parents
el dentista	the dentist
el tío	the uncle
la tía	the aunt
los tíos	the uncle and aunt
viejo/a	old
un viejo	an old person
el abuelo	the grandfather
la abuela	the grandmother
los abuelos	the grandparents
vivir	to live

Diálogo

María	Mira, Juan, ésta es una foto de mi familia.
Juan	¿Quién es esta mujer?
María	Es mi madre. Se llama Isabel.
Juan	Es guapa, ¿verdad?
María	Sí, es guapa, y también muy simpática.
Juan	Y éste es tu padre, ¿no?
María	Sí. Se llama José. Es dentista.
Juan	Y estas dos personas mayores son tus abuelos, ¿verdad?
María	Sí. Este es mi abuelo, y ésta es mi abuela.
Juan	¿Quién es este hombre con el pelo corto?
María	Es mi tío. Se llama Manuel. Y esta mujer es mi tía. Viven en Valencia.

Ejercicios

Cross reference with units: 1 12 23 32

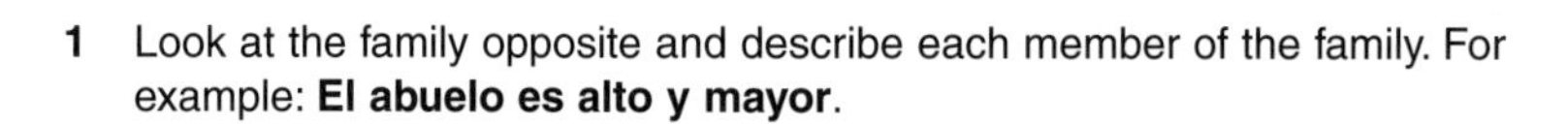

1 Look at the family opposite and describe each member of the family. For example: **El abuelo es alto y mayor**.

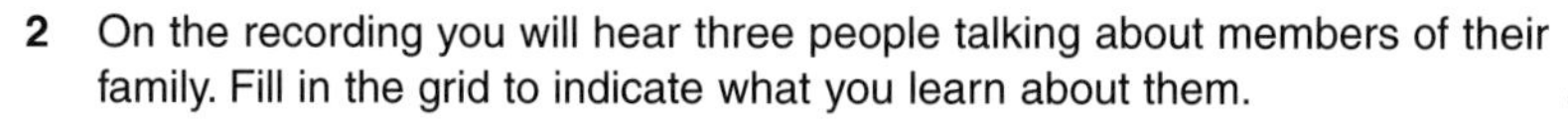

2 On the recording you will hear three people talking about members of their family. Fill in the grid to indicate what you learn about them.

Relation	Names	Ages	Characteristics
1.			
2.			
3.			

3 Question your Spanish friend about a family photograph.

(a) Ask who this man is. (b) Say he is short; isn't he? (c) Ask how old he is.
(d) Ask if he is pleasant. (e) Ask what the lady is called.

Lenguaje

To express 'they' (the 3rd person plural form) of regular verbs you add **-an** or **-en** to the stem of the verb.

comprar	to buy	**comprender**	to understand	**vivir**	to live
compran	they buy	**comprenden**	they understand	**viven**	they live

This form is used with **ustedes** to express 'you' plural in formal speech.

ustedes compran **ustedes comprenden** **ustedes viven**

La vida española

The use of the masculine plural to refer to members of the family, first referred to in Unit 12, continues with all members of the family. Therefore **los abuelos** are grandparents, **los tíos** are uncles and aunts, **los hermanos** are brothers and sisters, etc.

In the hotel

Making complaints about a hotel room

Vocabulario básico

el portero	the porter, waiter
ocurrir	to happen, occur
¿qué ocurre?	what's happening?
parecer	to seem
me parece que …	it seems to me that …
la sábana	the sheet
sucio/a	dirty
limpio/a	clean
la toalla	the towel
¡cuánto lo siento!	I'm so sorry
funcionar	to work (*of machines*)
la lámpara	the lamp
la mesa	the table
limpiar	to clean

Diálogo

Mujer ¡Oiga, señor! ¿Quiere venir un momento?
Portero Sí, señora. ¿Qué ocurre?
Mujer Me parece que esta sábana está sucia.
Portero Lo siento, señora. Voy a cambiar la sábana en seguida.
Mujer Y la toalla en el cuarto de baño no está limpia.
Portero Voy a traer toallas limpias en seguida, señora. ¿Alguna cosa más que no está bien?
Mujer Sí, la lámpara en la mesa no funciona.
Portero ¡Cuánto lo siento, señora! Voy a traer otra lámpara inmediatamente.
Mujer Gracias.

Ejercicios

1 Match the labels to the pictures, writing down the number of the picture and the letter of the label.

1. 
2. 
3. 
4. 
5. 
6. 

______ ______ ______ ______ ______ ______

(a) **La ducha**. (b) **La llave**. (c) **La toalla**. (d) **La sábana**. (e) **La lámpara**. (f) **El baño**.

Cross reference with units:

25

2 On the recording three people are making complaints about their hotel room. Select the sentence from those given below which best describes each person's complaint.

1. (a) The towel in the bathroom is dirty and the telephone does not work.
   (b) The bed is dirty and the shower does not work.
   (c) The towel in the bathroom is dirty and the television does not work.
2. (a) The bath is very dirty and the telephone does not work.
   (b) The shower is very dirty and the telephone does not work.
   (c) The sheets are dirty and the lamp does not work.
3. (a) The bed is dirty and the lamp does not work.
   (b) The shower is very dirty and the lamp does not work.
   (c) The shower does not work and the towels are dirty.

3 Recreate the dialogue on the facing page, using the following cues. You have sent for the porter, who will begin the conversation. (*Answers on pages 129–30.*)

- Tell him the sheet seems to be dirty.
- And the television doesn't work.
- Yes, the lamp on the table doesn't work.

Lenguaje

You saw in Unit 3 that the verb **estar** is used to indicate position.

¿Dónde está el bar?	Where is the bar?

It is also used to indicate a *temporary condition* such as being clean or dirty.

La toalla está sucia.	The towel is dirty.
La habitación está limpia.	The room is clean.

The verb **funcionar** is used to express 'work' of anything mechanical.

El teléfono no funciona.	The telephone is not working.
Mi coche funciona muy bien.	My car is going very well.

La vida española

In Spain it is quite normal to attract someone's attention with the order **¡Oiga!** plus a courtesy title, **¡Oiga, señorita!**

This can be followed by the polite request **¿Quiere venir un momento?** or **¿Quiere decirme a qué hora sale el próximo tren para Madrid?**

Making plans

Arranging a visit to a famous Spanish town

Vocabulario básico

¿le gustaría?	would you like?
conmigo	with me
que viene	next (*of time*)
me gustaría mucho	I would like very much
romano	Roman
el anfiteatro	the amphitheatre
el templo	the temple

Diálogo

Hombre	¿Le gustaría visitar Mérida conmigo el domingo que viene?
Mujer	Sí, me gustaría mucho.
Hombre	Muy bien.
Mujer	¿Es una ciudad interesante?
Hombre	Sí, es una ciudad histórica.
Mujer	¿Qué hay de interés?
Hombre	Pues, hay el teatro romano, el anfiteatro romano y el templo de Diana.
Mujer	¿A qué hora quiere usted salir?
Hombre	Si salimos de aquí a las nueve, podemos llegar a las once.
Mujer	Muy bien. Hasta el domingo que viene.
Hombre	Adiós. Hasta el domingo.

Ejercicios

1 Answer the questions, taking your cues from the ticks or crosses. (✔ = **me gustaría**; ✔✔ = **me gustaría mucho**; ✘ = **no me gustaría**)

1. ¿Le gustaría vivir en España? ✔
2. ¿Le gustaría tener mucho dinero? ✔✔
3. ¿Le gustaría trabajar en un hospital? ✘
4. ¿Le gustaría comer bien? ✔

2 On the recording, people are planning an outing. Fill in the grid below to indicate what they intend to do.

Place to visit	Day	Interesting sights
1.		
2.		

3 Recreate the dialogue on the facing page, using the verbal cues to help you.

- Say you would like to very much.
- Ask if it is an interesting town.
- Ask what there is of interest.
- Ask at what time he wishes to leave.
- Say 'Goodbye. Until Sunday.'

Lenguaje

To say 'I would like to' use **gustar** in what is known as the conditional tense.

¿Le gustaría visitar Mérida? Sí, me gustaría mucho.
Would you like to visit Mérida? Yes, I would like that very much.

'Next' in time is expressed by **... que viene** after the day, month or year, e.g. **la semana que viene**, 'next week'.

Voy a visitar Madrid el año que viene. I'm going to visit Madrid next year.

La vida española

The Roman theatre at Mérida was built by Agrippa in 24 BC. It can seat 6,000 people, and is still used for theatre and concerts. The Roman amphitheatre dates from the first century BC and can seat 14,000 spectators. The Temple of Diana, with its tall fluted columns, was joined to a house but has now been made free-standing.

Goods and services

Buying postcards and stamps

Vocabulario básico

vender	to sell
se venden	are sold
¿cuánto valen?	how much are ...?
la tarjeta postal	the postcard
el quiosco	the kiosk
allí	there
el sello	the stamp
Correos	the Post Office (*short for* **La Oficina de Correos**)
mandar	to send

Diálogos

En la calle

Turista	Perdón, señor. ¿Dónde se venden las tarjetas postales?
Transeúnte	Se venden en el quiosco, señora.
Turista	Y, ¿hay un quiosco por aquí?
Transeúnte	Sí, señora, allí hay uno, al otro lado de la calle.
Turista	Gracias, señor.

En el quiosco

Turista	¿Cuánto valen las tarjetas postales?
Vendedor	Valen treinta pesetas cada una, señora.
Turista	Estas seis, por favor.
Vendedor	Son ciento ochenta pesetas, señora.
Turista	Aquí tiene usted. ¿Los sellos se venden aquí?
Vendedor	No, señora, los sellos se venden en Correos.

En Correos

Turista	¿Cuánto vale mandar una tarjeta postal a Inglaterra?
Empleado	Vale cincuenta y cinco pesetas, señora.
Turista	Déme seis sellos de cincuenta y cinco pesetas.
Empleado	Aquí tiene usted. Trescientas treinta pesetas.
Turista	Aquí tiene usted.

Ejercicios

1 Look at the shops shown below and answer the questions:

Cross reference with units:

1. ¿Dónde se venden las naranjas?
2. ¿Dónde se vende la carne?
3. ¿Dónde se compran los sellos?
4. ¿Dónde se compra la leche?

2 On the recording three people are finding out where things are sold.
Fill in the grid to show what each person wants and where it is to be found.

Thing needed	Place it is found	Where is it?
1.		
2.		
3.		

3 Recreate the dialogue on the facing page, using the verbal cues to help you. (*Answers on page 130.*)

- Ask how much the postcards cost.
- Say 'These five, please.'
- Say 'Here you are.' Ask if stamps are sold there.
- Ask how you get to the Post Office.

Lenguaje

In Unit 27 you saw the form for the passive voice. **Y, ¿se fabrica por aquí?** 'And is it made around here?' You can use this form with virtually every Spanish verb in two forms:

¿Dónde se cultiva el arroz? Where is rice grown?
¿Dónde se cultivan las naranjas? Where are oranges grown?

You may often hear **Eso no se hace**, 'That is not done', or **Eso no se dice**, 'That is not said.

La vida española

Postal services in Spain are found in **Correos** (mail), which is a short form of **La Oficina de Correos**. You therefore ask: **¿Dónde está Correos, por favor?**
El estanco (tobacconist) also sells stamps, newspapers and tobacco products and is state-owned.

Food and drink

Getting further portions of food and drink

Vocabulario básico

la esposa	the wife
tener sed, hambre, calor, frío	to be thirsty, hungry, hot, cold
¿qué tiene de ...?	what have you got for ...?
el flan	the caramel custard
la nata	the cream
la tarta helada	ice-cream cake
el melocotón	the peach
la uva	the grape

Diálogo

Cliente	¡Camarera!
Camarera	¿Señor?
Cliente	¿Quiere traerme más pan?
Camarera	En seguida, señor.
Cliente	Mi esposa tiene sed. Tráigame una botella de agua mineral.
Camarera	¿Con gas o sin gas?
Cliente	Sin gas.
Camarera	Muy bien. ¿Toman ustedes postre?
Cliente	¿Qué tiene de postre?
Camarera	Pues, hay flan con nata, tarta helada, melocotón, uvas ...
Cliente	Un flan con nata para mí y un melocotón para mi esposa.
Camarera	En seguida, señor.

Ejercicios

1 What does the customer want more of? Match the labels to the pictures.

1

2

3

4

Labels:
(a) Una botella de vino.
(b) Pan.
(c) Patatas fritas.
(d) Una botella de agua mineral.

Cross reference with units:

2 On the recording two customers are asking for additional portions of something and a dessert. Mark the sentences below as TRUE or FALSE and try to correct the false ones.

1. More chips, a bottle of sparkling mineral water, chocolate ice-cream and grapes. __________
2. More bread, another bottle of white wine, caramel custard with cream, and cheese. __________

3 Recreate the dialogue on the facing page, using the verbal cues to help you. (*Answers on page 130.*)

- Call the waiter.
- Ask her to bring you some more chips.
- Say your son is thirsty. Say 'Bring me a bottle of mineral water.'
- Say fizzy.
- Say yes. Grapes for you and an ice-cream for your son.

Lenguaje

The verb **tener** is used with nouns to express hunger, thirst, feeling hot, feeling cold, etc.

Tengo hambre.	I'm hungry.
Tengo frío.	I'm cold.

The word **mucho**, **mucha** can also be used to mean 'very' in certain contexts when you are modifying a noun such as **calor**.

Tengo mucha sed.	I'm very thirsty.
Tengo mucho calor.	I'm very hot.

La vida española

Restaurants with three forks or more normally offer an English version of the menu. It is often preferable to use the Spanish menu, because the translation can be misleading. Restaurants in tourist areas offer **Platos combinados**, which are complete meals served on one plate. Tipping is still customary in Spanish restaurants, and it is normal to add 10 per cent to the bill.

Travel

Travel by bus and coach

Vocabulario básico

el autocar	the coach (*travel between towns, and excursions*)
para	for (destined for)
pasa por	it passes through
directamente	directly
coja	catch, get on
baje	get off (*order*)
cruce	cross (*order*)
suba	go up (*order*)

Diálogos

En la parada del autobús

Mujer Perdón. ¿Es éste el autobús para la Plaza Mayor?
Hombre No, señora. Éste va a la estación de ferrocarriles.
Mujer Pero, pasa por la Plaza Mayor, ¿verdad?
Hombre No, señora. Va directamente a la estación.
Mujer ¿Cuál es el autobús para la Plaza Mayor?
Hombre Creo que es el número quince.
Mujer ¿De dónde sale? ¿De aquí?
Hombre No. Sale de esa parada al otro lado de la calle.
Mujer Gracias.

En el autobús

Mujer Perdón. ¿Dónde bajo para la Plaza Mayor?
Hombre Baje en la próxima parada.
Mujer Y, ¿la Plaza Mayor está cerca?
Hombre Sí, señora. Cruce la calle, suba por la calle del Arenal y está en la Plaza Mayor.
Mujer Gracias.

Ejercicios

1 What are you going to do if you receive these instructions?

(a) Coja el autobús número tres, y baje en la cuarta parada.
(b) Baje en la próxima parada, cruce la calle y ahí está el teatro.
(c) Coja el autobús número diez y baje en la Plaza Mayor. Ahí está el Banco Central.

2 On the recording two people are asking about buses. Fill in the grid below.

Destination	Other information given
1.	
2.	

Cross reference with units:

3 Ask a Spanish passer-by if:

(a) This is the bus for the railway station.
(b) Which is the bus for the railway station.
(c) Where does the bus leave from.
(d) Is the railway station nearby.

Lenguaje

Adverbs describe verbs. In English they often end in '-ly' – slowly, badly. To form most adverbs in Spanish you add **-mente** to the feminine form of the adjective:

rápido – rápida – rápidamente	quickly

If the adjective does not have a feminine form (and adjectives which end in anything other than **-o** do not), the form is:

fácil – fácilmente	easily

Common irregular adverbs are:

deprisa	quickly
despacio	slowly
bien	well
mal	badly
tarde	late
temprano	early

La vida española

In big cities you pay the driver on a bus, or purchase a **bonobús**, a ticket valid for ten journeys, which you punch in a machine as you board the bus.

In some cities there are swift bus services provided by **microbuses**, which start from the city outskirts and go directly to the city centre without stopping.

Free time

Talking about your favourite pastimes

Vocabulario básico

favorito	favourite
el windsurf	windsurfing
encantar	to love, be very keen on
peligroso	dangerous
¡qué va!	rubbish! nonsense!
emocionante	exciting
el lago	the lake
la película	the film
el idioma	the language
extranjero	foreign
saber (+ infinitive)	to know how to do something
sé . . .	I can . . .
hablar	to speak
el francés	French (*both the language and a person*)

Diálogo

Juan ¿Cuál es tu pasatiempo favorito, María?
María Me encanta el windsurf.
Juan ¿No es un deporte peligroso?
María ¡Qué va! Es muy emocionante.
Juan ¿Dónde practicas el windsurf?
María En la playa o en un lago cerca de mi casa.
Juan ¿Sabes nadar?
María Claro. Sé nadar muy bien. ¿Qué te gusta a ti?
Juan Me encantan las películas extranjeras.
María ¿Comprendes los idiomas extranjeros?
Juan Claro. Sé hablar el francés y el inglés muy bien.

Ejercicios

1 Follow the lines to find out what each person loves to do. For example: **A Juan le encanta el windsurf**.

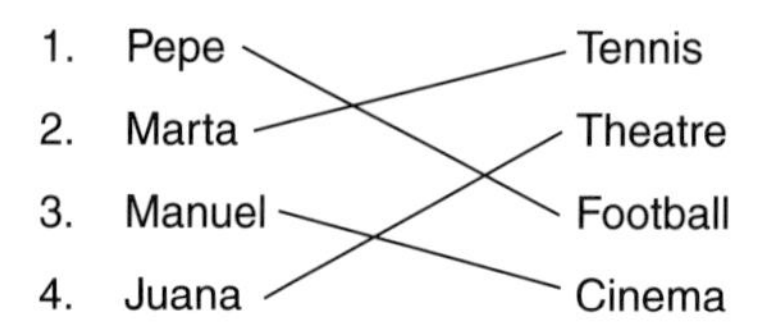

Cross reference with units: 8 19 21 30

2 On the recording three people are talking about their favourite pastime. Fill in the grid below.

Favourite activity	Other information
1.	
2.	
3.	

3 These are the answers, but, what were the questions?

(a) Me encanta el windsurf.
(b) En un lago cerca de mi casa.
(c) SÍ, sé nadar muy bien.
(d) ¿Sí, sé hablar italiano e inglés muy bien.

Lenguaje

The verb **encantar** behaves like **gustar**. You only use two forms, **encanta** and **encantan**, and change the pronoun before the verb to indicate the person.

Me encanta el tenis.	I love tennis.
Me encantan las vacaciones.	I love holidays.
Te encanta la televisión.	You love television (*to a friend, etc.*).
Te encantan las novelas románticas.	You love romantic novels.

La vida española

Spanish, like other languages, 'borrows' words and sometimes gets them slightly wrong. **El windsurf** for 'windsurfing' is a good example.

Other examples are: **hacer footing**, 'to go jogging'; **el wáter** or **el váter**, 'lavatory' (*from* 'water closet'); **un champú**, 'a shampoo'; **un crismas**, 'a Christmas card'; **un esmoquin**, 'a dinner jacket' and **un lifting**, 'a facelift'.

Talking about the past

Describing a visit to a famous town

Vocabulario básico

usted pasó	you spent
¿le gustó?	did you like?
me gustó	I liked
compré	I bought
usted compró	you bought
la estatua	the statue
saqué fotos	I took photos
usted sacó fotos	you took photos
costó	it cost

Diálogo

Mujer	¿Dónde pasó usted el fin de semana?
Hombre	Visité Mérida con mi amiga.
Mujer	¿Le gustó?
Hombre	Sí, me gustó mucho.
Mujer	¿Sacó usted muchas fotos?
Hombre	Sí, saqué fotos del teatro romano.
Mujer	Y, ¿compró usted algún recuerdo?
Hombre	Sí, compré esta pequeña estatua romana.
Mujer	¿Costó mucho la estatua?
Hombre	No, sólo mil pesetas.

Ejercicios

1 Trace the lines and say where each person went and what they bought. For example:

José visitó Madrid y compró unas gafas de sol.

José

1.

María

2.

Rafael

3.

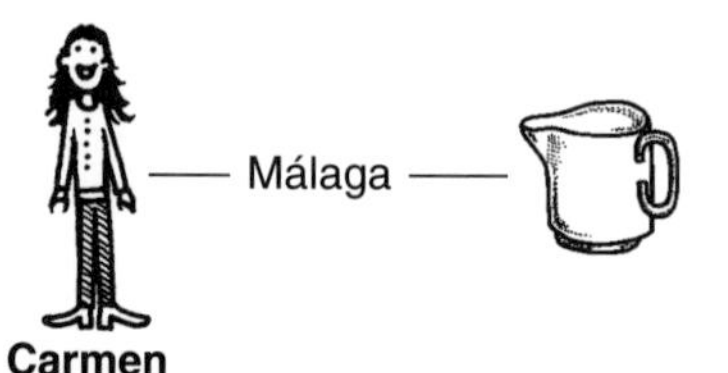

Carmen

4.

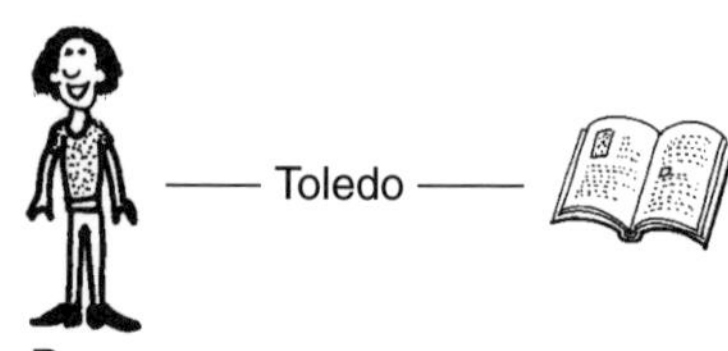

Pepe

2 ¿Qué se dice? (What does one say?) What are the questions to obtain the following information?

(a) Where did you spend the weekend?
(b) Did you like it?
(c) Did you take a lot of photos?
(d) Did you buy any souvenirs?
(e) Did it cost a lot?

3 Take part in the dialogue on the facing page, using the cues below to help you. (*Answers on page 130.*)

- Answer the question by saying that you visited Madrid with a friend.
- Say that, yes, you liked it very much.
- Say that, yes, you took photos of the Prado Museum.
- Say that, yes, you bought this handbag.
- Say 'No, only 5.000 pesetas.'

Lenguaje

The simple past tense, called the preterite, is used to describe a single action in the past. For verbs ending in **-ar**, the 1st and 3rd persons singular are as follows:

comprar to buy

Compré un recuerdo.	I bought a souvenir.
Juan compró un disco.	John bought a record.
Usted compró un bolso.	You bought a handbag. (*formal speech*)

To express what you liked, in this tense, you always use **gustó** preceded by the relevant pronoun.

me gustó	I liked
le gustó	he/she liked
te gustó	you liked (*informal*)
¿Le gustó Mérida?	Did you like Mérida?
Sí, me gustó mucho.	Yes, I liked it a lot.

La vida española

Taking photographs of interesting people in Spain is an important part of the holiday to many tourists, but you should be aware of the feelings of the subjects. They may simply be going about their daily work and may resent the intrusion of your camera. If you show them the camera and simply say: **¿Se puede ...?** ('May I ...?') you will rarely be refused permission.

The weather

Talking about what is possible

Vocabulario básico

dime	tell me (*talking to a friend*)
¿Se puede?	can I? Is it allowed? (*lit.* Can one?)
el viento	the wind
hace viento	it's windy
agradable	pleasant, agreeable
mejor	better, best
la estación	the season
prohibido	prohibited
está prohibido	it's prohibited
el río	the river

Diálogo

María Dime, Juan, ¿se puede practicar el windsurf todo el año?
Juan Si hace viento, sí, se puede.
María Pero, cuando hace mucho frío, ¿se puede practicar el windsurf?
Juan Es menos agradable, claro, pero se puede.
María ¿Cuál es la mejor estación para el windsurf?
Juan Es mejor en el verano cuando hace sol.
María ¿Se puede practicar el windsurf en el río?
Juan No, no se puede. Está prohibido.
María ¡Qué lástima! El río está muy cerca de tu casa.
Juan Sí, es verdad.

Ejercicios

1 Look at the notices and decide what is prohibited.

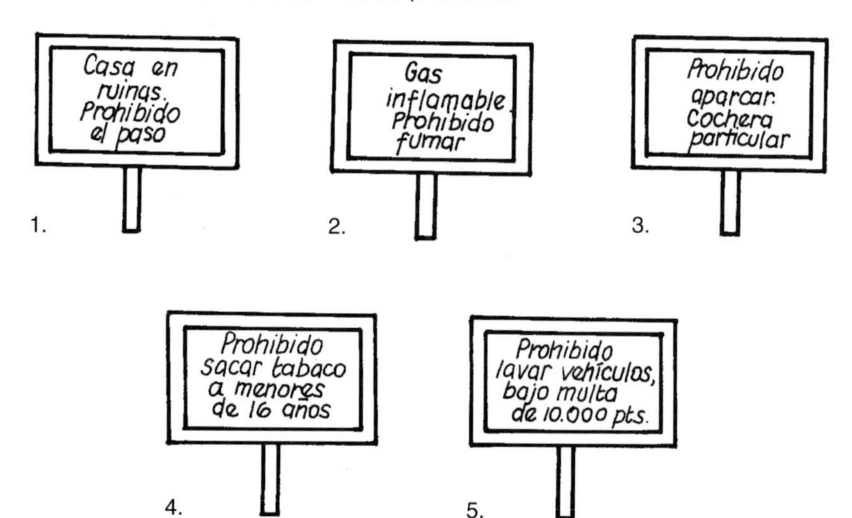

Cross reference with units: 9 31

2 On the recording you will hear what is prohibited and what is allowed. Mark the activities with a tick if the activity is allowed, or a cross if it is prohibited, as you hear them, and fill in the gap for the sixth activity.

1. Park a car.
2. Play golf in the park.
3. Take photos.
4. Swim in the lake.
5. Smoke in the restaurant.
6. __________________.

3 ¿Se puede o no se puede? (Can you or can't you?) Give reasonable answers to these questions.

a) ¿Se puede practicar el windsurf en casa?
b) ¿Se puede practicar el tenis cuando hace sol?
c) ¿Se puede esquiar cuando hace mucho calor?
d) ¿Se puede aparcar fácilmente en su ciudad?
e) ¿Se puede fumar en el cine en Inglaterra?

Lenguaje

Mejor expresses 'better', and allows you to make comparisons.

El vino es mejor que la cerveza.	Wine is better than beer.

To express 'best' you simply place the definite article, **el**, **la**, **los**, **las**, before **mejor**.

Éste es el mejor restaurante de la ciudad.	This is the best restaurant in the town.

La vida española

Con permiso ('with your permission') or **¿Se puede ...?** will allow you to ask to do most things in Spain. For example, if you need another chair at your café table and there is one free at an adjacent table, you merely approach the people at the other table, gesture to the chair and say **Con permiso** or **¿Se puede ...?** This simple phrase conveys the clear message that you wish to take the chair.

Unit 43 Emergencies

Reporting a theft from your car to the police

Vocabulario básico

la comisaría	the police station
el policía	the policeman
denunciar	to report
el robo	the theft
hace (+ time)	. . . ago
hace media hora	half an hour ago
el parking	the car-park
robar	to steal
la radio	the radio
la marca	the brand
la maleta	the suitcase
la ropa	the clothes
estar de vacaciones	to be on holiday
los detalles	the details
las herramientas	the tools

Diálogo

Policía	Buenas tardes, señora. ¿En qué puedo servirle?
Mujer	Quiero denunciar un robo.
Policía	¿Cuándo ocurrió el robo?
Mujer	Hace una hora.
Policía	Y, ¿dónde ocurrió?
Mujer	En el parking del Hotel Castilla.
Policía	¿Qué robó el ladrón exactamente?
Mujer	Una radio y una maleta.
Policía	¿De qué marca es la radio?
Mujer	Es la radio del coche, una Sony.
Policía	Y, ¿qué hay en la maleta?
Mujer	Ropa. Estoy de vacaciones.
Policía	Muy bien. ¿Quiere darme más detalles?
Mujer	Claro. Pues ...

Ejercicios

1 Follow the lines and say what the thief stole and where he stole it. For example:

El ladrón robó una radio de un coche en el parking.

Cross reference with units:

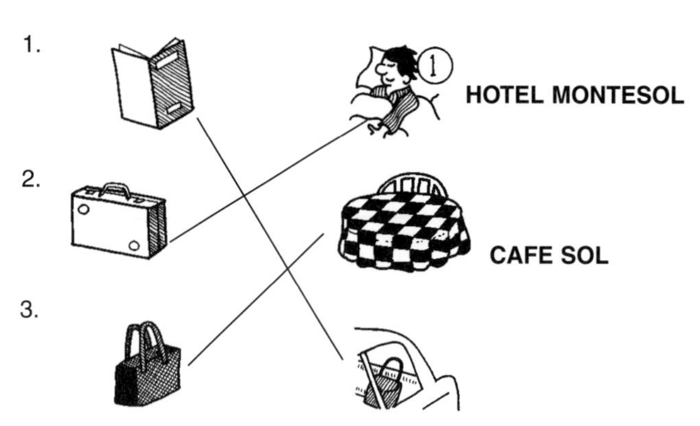

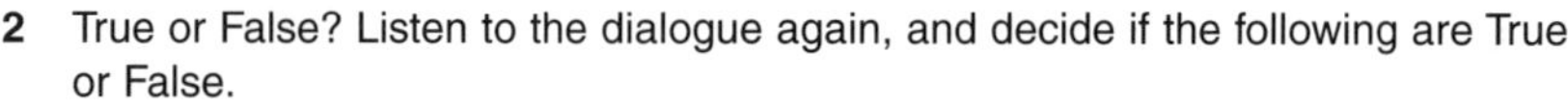

2 True or False? Listen to the dialogue again, and decide if the following are True or False.

a) The woman wants to report an accident.
b) It happened an hour ago.
c) It happened in the bar of the Hotel Castilla.
d) The thief stole money and a passport.
e) The woman is on holiday.

3 Recreate the dialogue on the facing page using the cues below to help you. (*Answers on page 130.*)

- Say 'I want to report a robbery.'
- Say 'Half an hour ago.'
- Say 'In the hotel bedroom.'
- Say 'A handbag.'
- Say 'Money and my passport.'

Lenguaje

The simple past or preterite of verbs which end in **-er** or **-ir** in the singular is as follows:

-er		-ir	
Comí bien.	I ate well.	**Salí a las ocho.**	I left at 8.
Comiste mucho.	You ate a lot.	**Saliste a las dos.**	You left at 2.
Comió en casa.	He/She ate at home.	**Salío a la una.**	He/She left at 1.
Usted comió mal.	You ate badly.	**Usted salió tarde.**	You left late.

La vida española

Unfortunately, theft from tourists' cars is all too common in Spain, and cars with foreign number-plates are particularly vulnerable. The safest place for your car is in the hotel car-park, which will have attendants. An **Aparcamiento vigilado** in town will give you the same protection.

Goods and services

Discussing a shopping trip with a friend

Vocabulario básico

ir de compras	to go shopping
¿fuiste de compras?	did you go shopping?
fui de compras	I went shopping
pasado/a	last (*in time*)
aquel/aquella	that (*far from both speakers*)
la tienda de modas	the boutique, dress shop
compraste	you bought
costaron	they cost
el vestido	the dress
elegante	elegant
la ganga	the bargain

Diálogo

Manuel ¿Fuiste de compras el sábado pasado, Isabel?
Isabel Sí, fui a Moderama.
Manuel ¿Dónde está?
Isabel Es aquella tienda de modas en la Plaza Mayor.
Manuel ¿Compraste algo?
Isabel Sí, compré este vestido. ¿Te gusta?
Manuel Sí, es muy elegante. ¿Te costó mucho?
Isabel No. Sólo diez mil pesetas.
Manuel Una ganga, ¿no, Isabel?
Isabel Sí, es verdad. Una ganga.

Ejercicios

1 Look at the pictures, say where you went and what you bought. For example:

Fui a la frutería y compré dos kilos de manzanas.

1. 

2. 

3. 

Cross reference with units: 5 16 26 27 37

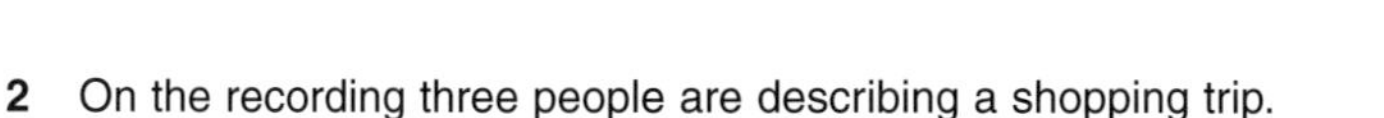

2 On the recording three people are describing a shopping trip. On the grid below fill in what they did.

When	Where	Purchases	Price
1.			
2.			
3.			

3 Ask your friend about a shopping trip. Ask:

a) Did you go shopping last week?
b) Where is that shop?
c) Did you buy anything?
d) Did it cost a lot?
e) A bargain, no?

Lenguaje

The verb **ir**, 'to go', does not follow the pattern given in Unit 43 and must be learned separately. The past tense is as follows:

Fui a Madrid.	I went to Madrid.
Fuiste de compras.	You went shopping.
Fue a Toledo.	He/She went to Toledo.
Usted fue a la oficina.	You went to the office.

La vida española

Shops in Spain are generally open from 10.00 a.m. to 13.30, and from 17.00 to 20.00. Some department stores stay open all day. The most famous department store is **El Corte Inglés**, and it has branches in most Spanish cities. Many have telephones with national flags above them. If you pick up the phone with the American flag, an assistant who speaks American English will come to help you.

UNIT 45 My family and I

Talking about yourself, your children and grandchildren

Vocabulario básico

los Estados Unidos	the United States
¿de veras?	really? is that so?
el profesor	the teacher
los nietos	the grandchildren
el nieto	the grandson
la nieta	the granddaughter
soltero/a	unmarried
jubilado/a	retired

Diálogo

Hombre ¿Está usted casada?
Mujer Sí, estoy casada.
Hombre ¿Tiene usted hijos?
Mujer Sí, tengo dos; un hijo y una hija.
Hombre Y, ¿viven con usted?
Mujer Pues hace cinco años mi hijo se fue a vivir a los Estados Unidos.
Hombre ¿De veras? ¿A qué parte de los Estados Unidos?
Mujer A Nueva York.
Hombre Y, ¿trabaja allí?
Mujer Sí, es profesor de español en la universidad de Nueva York.
Hombre ¿Tiene usted nietos?
Mujer Sí, tengo tres; dos nietos y una nieta.
Hombre ¿Está casada su hija?
Mujer No, es soltera, y vive conmigo.
Hombre ¿Trabaja su marido?
Mujer No. Está jubilado.

Ejercicios

1 Look at the family tree given opposite and answer the questions on the next page.

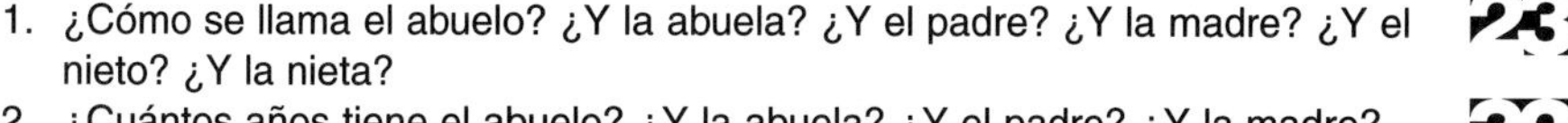

Cross reference with units:

1. ¿Cómo se llama el abuelo? ¿Y la abuela? ¿Y el padre? ¿Y la madre? ¿Y el nieto? ¿Y la nieta?
2. ¿Cuántos años tiene el abuelo? ¿Y la abuela? ¿Y el padre? ¿Y la madre? ¿Y el nieto? ¿Y la nieta?
3. ¿En qué trabaja la abuela? ¿Y el abuelo? ¿Y la madre? ¿Y el padre?

2 On the recording three people are discussing their civil status and their children or grandchildren. Mark the following statements TRUE or FALSE and correct the false ones.

1. She is married with two children. ______________
2. He is married with one daughter who is a schoolteacher. ______________
3. He is married with three grandchildren. He is retired. ______________

3 ¿**Es** o **está**? Fill in the gaps with **es** or **está**?

1. Madrid . . . . . en el centro de España.
2. Madrid . . . . . la capital de España.
3. Mi hija . . . . . casada y tiene tres hijos.
4. ¿Cómo . . . . . usted? Muy bien, gracias.
5. Mi hijo. . . . . arquitecto y trabaja en Madrid.

Lenguaje

The verb **estar** is used to express three areas of language.

1. Position

¿Dónde está Madrid? Where is Madrid?

2. Temporary condition

¿Cómo está usted? Estoy muy bien. How are you? I'm very well.

3. A state which results from an action

Me casé. I got married. (action)
Estoy casado. I'm married. (result)

But: **Soy soltero/a.** I'm unmarried. (no action)

This last use of the verb explains why you should say: **Está muerto**, 'He's dead'.

La vida española

Spanish is a truly international language, spoken in Spain and twenty countries in South America. Spanish is also widely spoken in the United States, where some 7 per cent of the population, or 15,000,000 persons, have Spanish as their native language. There are also sizeable Spanish-speaking groups in the Philippines and Israel.

Unit 46 Emergencies

In the doctor's surgery

Vocabulario básico

vamos a ver	let's see
¿qué le duele?	what's hurting you?
me duele la cabeza	I've got a headache
me duelen los ojos	my eyes hurt
dormir	to sleep
ayer	yesterday
el grado	degree (*of heat*)
el pie	the foot
la mano	the hand
grave	serious
no se preocupe	don't worry (*order*)
no vuelva	don't go back (*order*)
una insolación	sunstroke
la consulta	the doctor's surgery

Diálogo

Doctora	Vamos a ver, señor López. ¿Qué le duele?
López	Me duele mucho la cabeza, doctora.
Doctora	¿La cabeza? ¿Algo más?
López	Me duelen bastante los ojos.
Doctora	¿Cuánto tiempo pasó usted en la playa ayer?
López	Tres horas, doctora.
Doctora	Mucho calor ayer en la playa, ¿verdad?
López	Sí, más de treinta grados. ¿Es grave?
Doctora	No. No se preocupe. Es un poco de insolación.
López	¿Qué tengo que hacer?
Doctora	Tome dos aspirinas cada tres horas, y no vuelva a la playa.

Ejercicios

1 Label as many parts of the body as you know: **la cabeza**; **el estómago**; **la garganta**; **la muela**; **el ojo**; **la mano**; **el pie**.

Cross reference with units: 11 22 43

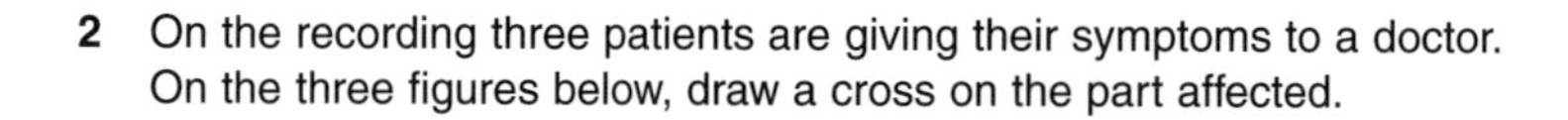

2 On the recording three patients are giving their symptoms to a doctor. On the three figures below, draw a cross on the part affected.

3 Recreate the dialogue on the facing page. (*Answers on page 131.*)

- Say your head hurts a lot.
- Say that you have a sore throat.
- You were there for four hours.
- Say yes, more than 30 degrees. Ask if it is serious.
- Ask what you must do.

Lenguaje

To express illness, you use the verb **doler**, which has two forms in the present tense, **duele** and **duelen**.

If what hurts is singular, you use **duele**.

Me duele la cabeza. I've got a headache.

If what hurts is plural, you use **duelen**.

Me duelen los pies. My feet hurt.

Therefore the doctor may ask you: **¿Qué le duele?** 'What's hurting you?' If you cannot remember the Spanish for the part of the body which is hurting, you can point to the offending spot and say: **Me duele aquí**, 'It's hurting here.' At least the doctor will know where to start!

La vida española

If you are British and travel to Spain, you should obtain Form E111 from the DSS before you go. This will entitle you to urgent treatment for accident or illness in EC countries. Doctors usually display their surgery hours outside the premises as **Horas de consulta**.

UNIT 47

In the hotel

Settling your bill in a hotel

Vocabulario básico

¿qué significa?	what does it mean?
la bodega	drinks (*on hotel bill*), (*often*) wine-cellar
la bebida	the drink
el comedor	the dining-room
¿acepta usted?	do you accept?
personal	personal
el eurocheque	the Eurocheque
el recibo	the receipt
la llamada internacional	international phone-call

Diálogo

Cliente	La cuenta de la habitación número diez, por favor.
Recepcionista	Muy bien. Un momento, por favor.
Recepcionista	Aquí tiene usted.
Cliente	No comprendo esto. ¿Qué significa 'bodega'?
Recepcionista	Son las bebidas que tomó usted en el comedor.
Cliente	Ah, muy bien. ¿Acepta usted un cheque personal?
Recepcionista	No, señor. Sólo eurocheques o tarjetas de crédito.
Cliente	Bueno, entonces una tarjeta de crédito American Express.
Recepcionista	Gracias, señor. Aquí tiene usted el recibo.
Cliente	Gracias.

Ejercicios

1 Here are the answers. What were the questions? For example:
Me llamo Paco. = ¿Cómo se llama usted?

(a) Tengo treinta y dos años. (b) Es verde. (c) El tren sale a las diez y media. (d) Hay treinta y tres alumnos en la clase. (e) Me llamo Roberto.

2 On the recording three customers are settling their bills. Fill in the grid.

Room number	Word not understood	Word meaning	Method of payment
1.			
2.			
3.			

Cross reference with units:

3 ¿Qué significa? (What does it mean?) Use what you have learned about Spanish to guess the meaning of the words in **bold**.

1. Me gusta mucho la cama. Soy muy **dormilón (dormilona)**.
2. Me encanta comer bien. Soy bastante **comilón (comilona)**.
3. Me gusta mucho hablar con la gente. Soy muy **hablador (habladora)**.
4. Me gustan mucho todos los vinos españoles. Soy **bebedor (bebedora)**.

Lenguaje

If you do not understand something, you say **No comprendo esto**. If you want to ask what the word means, you ask **¿Qué significa ...?**

No comprendo ésto. ¿Qué significa 'llamadas interurbanas'?
I don't understand this. What does 'long-distance calls' mean?

Vale has two different meanings. It is used to ask a price.

¿Cuánto vale este bolso? How much is this handbag?

It is also used to indicate asking for and getting agreement.

Mañana a las diez en la plaza, ¿vale? Vale. Tomorrow at 10 in the square, OK? OK.

La vida española

In a Spanish hotel, **pensión completa** means 'full board', **media pensión** indicates 'half board' and **desayuno incluido** tells you that breakfast is included in the price of the room. **Camas, sólo dormir** is the sign for the cheapest, student-like accommodation.

Talking about the past

Reporting on a business trip

Vocabulario básico

la visita	the visit
la feria	the fair
comercial	commercial, business
había	there was, were
el stand	stand (*at fair*)
recibí	I received
el pedido	the order (*commercial*)
el ordenador	the computer
el software	the software
más de	more than (*with numbers*)
un millón	a million
el procesador de textos	the word processor
en total	in all, in total

Diálogo

Manuel	¿Qué tal la visita a Barcelona?
Marta	Muy bien. Fui a la Feria Comercial.
Manuel	¿Había mucho interés en el stand?
Marta	Sí, recibí muchos pedidos para el nuevo ordenador.
Manuel	¿Y el software? ¿Había también interés?
Marta	Sí, mucho. Más de cien pedidos.
Manuel	¿Recibió pedidos para el procesador de textos?
Marta	También. En total más de veinte millones de pesetas.
Manuel	¡Qué bien!

Ejercicios

1 Match the labels to the pictures, writing down the letter of the label and the number of the picture.

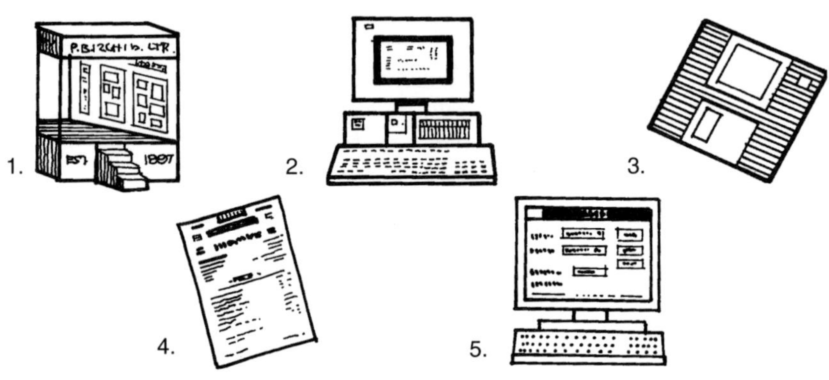

(a) **el pedido** (b) **el procesador de textos** (c) **el stand** (d) **el ordenador** (e) **el software**

2 Did you do well? Read the following and answer the questions in English.

(a) Recibí pedidos por más de cien millones de pesetas.
What was the value of the orders?
(b) Recibí pedidos por más de veinte millones de pesetas.
What was the value of the orders?
(c) Había mucho interés por las nuevas novelas.
What were people interested in?

3 Recreate the dialogue on the facing page, using the cues below to help you. (*Answers on page 131.*)

- Say 'Very good' and that you went to the Leather fair.
- Say that, yes, you received many orders for the new shoes.
- Say 'Yes, lots, more than 50 orders.'
- Say 'Yes. In total more than 30 million pesetas.

Lenguaje

Hay expresses 'there is' and 'there are'.

Hay muchos turistas en Sevilla. There are lots of tourists in Seville.

Había is the past tense of **hay**, and expresses 'there was' and 'there were'.

¿Había mucho interés? Was there a lot of interest?

Un millón expresses 'one million' and is followed by **de**. **Un millón de pesetas**, '1,000,000 pesetas'. The plural is **millones**.

Madrid tiene cuatro millones de habitantes. Madrid has 4,000,000 inhabitants.

La vida española

Information technology (*la informática*) borrows many words from English as can be seen from the vocabulary list. Can you guess the meanings of these other borrowed words? **Digital**; **disco flexible**; **hardware**; **memoria**; **microprocesador**; **editor de textos**.

My home town

Describing your ideal house

Vocabulario básico

ideal	ideal
la cocina	the kitchen, the stove, cooking
la nevera	the refrigerator
el lavaplatos	the dishwasher
el dormitorio	the bedroom (*in house*)
el armario	the wardrobe
la silla	the chair
el sofá	the sofa
la butaca	the armchair
la suerte	good luck

Diálogo

Isabel	Ayer compré mi casa ideal.
Juan	¿Dónde?
Isabel	En un pueblo cerca de Málaga.
Juan	¿Cómo es la casa?
Isabel	Es bastante grande. Tiene cuatro dormitorios.
Juan	¿Cómo es la cocina?
Isabel	Es muy bonita. Hay una cocina de gas, una nevera y un lavaplatos.
Juan	¿Qué hay en el comedor?
Isabel	Hay una mesa muy grande con seis sillas.
Juan	¿Es grande o pequeño el salón?
Isabel	Es grande, con un sofá, dos butacas y una televisión.
Juan	¡Qué suerte tienes, Isabel!

Ejercicios

1 Label the rooms and furniture in the house below.

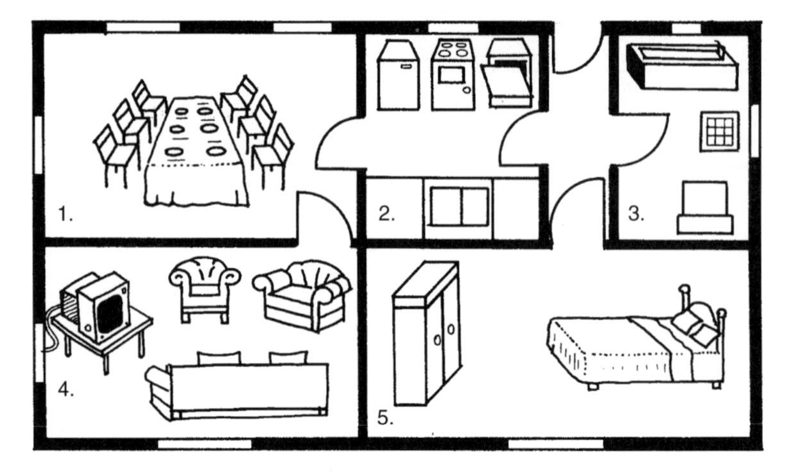

Cross reference with units:

2 On the recording three people are describing their ideal house. Fill in the grid to show what the houses are like.

Bedrooms	Kitchen contents	Living room contents
1.		
2.		
3.		

3 Sense or nonsense? Mark these sentences as being sensible or nonsensical.

1. Mi casa ideal está en Madrid cerca de Málaga.
2. En mi casa ideal la nevera está en el dormitorio.
3. Hay tres butacas muy cómodas en el salón.
4. El lavaplatos está en el cuarto de baño cerca de la ducha.
5. En el salón hay una cocina de gas, una nevera y una radio.

Lenguaje

La cocina has three distinct meanings in Spanish.

1. The kitchen **La cocina es muy bonita.** The kitchen is very nice.
2. The stove **Hay una cocina eléctrica.** There's an electric stove.
3. Cooking **La cocina española es muy buena.** Spanish cooking is very good.

'Chair' is expressed in two ways. **La silla** means 'dining-room chair' and **la butaca** means 'armchair' or 'stall' in a cinema or theatre.

La vida española

Many people dream of retiring to Spain, but buying property there can bring problems. You need a reliable English-speaking lawyer who will help you get the vital document **la escritura** (property deeds). To avoid the possible pitfalls of living in Spain, you should buy a book such as **Spanish Property Owner's Community Handbook**, by David Searl, published by Lookout, a publication for English-speakers living in Spain.

Finding your way

Finding your way in a Spanish town

Vocabulario básico

ayudar	to help
perdido/a	lost
busco	I'm looking for
¿qué hago?	what do I do?
la cita	the appointment, date
amable	kind
necesario	necessary
el Metro	the underground
como usted quiera	as you wish
la parada de taxis	taxi rank

Diálogo

Mujer ¿Puede ayudarme? Estoy perdida.
Hombre ¿Adónde quiere usted ir, señorita?
Mujer Busco el Hotel Pintor en la calle de Goya.
Hombre La calle de Goya está muy lejos, señorita.
Mujer ¿No está por aquí?
Hombre No, señorita, está a más de dos kilómetros.
Mujer ¿Qué hago? Tengo una cita en el hotel a las diez.
Hombre La llevo en mi coche. Ahí está.
Mujer No, gracias. Es usted muy amable.
Hombre Venga, señorita. No se preocupe.
Mujer No es necesario. Prefiero coger un taxi.
Hombre Como usted quiera, señorita.
Mujer Ahí viene uno. ¡Taxi! ¡Taxi!

Ejercicios

1 Unscramble the words in **bold** to find words to do with transport.

(a) Voy a coger el **nert** para visitar a mi amigo en Washington.
(b) El taxi me lleva a la **óscaneti** para coger el tren.
(c) Cuando voy al centro de la ciudad cojo el **stoubaú**.
(d) Quiero un **tielebl** de ida y vuleta, por favor.
(e) El tren para Nueva York está en el **nandé** número cinco.

2 On the recording two people are lost and are given advice to help them find their way. Fill in the grid below, giving their destination, the advice offered and what is preferred.

Destination	Location/distance	Advice offered	Transport chosen
1.			
2.			

3 Recreate the dialogue on the facing page, using the cues in the book to help you. (*Answers on page 131.*)

- Ask for help and say that you are lost.
- Say that you are looking for the Hotel Atlántico in Arenal Street.
- Ask 'what should I do?' Say that you have an appointment in the hotel at 5.
- Say that, no, you prefer to take a taxi.
- Say 'Here one comes. Taxi! Taxi!'

Lenguaje

To express 'to look *at*', you use the verb **mirar**.

Miro la plaza. I look at the square.

Buscar is used for 'to look for'.

Busco el Hotel Goya. I'm looking for Goya Hotel.

¿Qué hago? expresses the idea of 'What should I do?', even if it is the present tense.

Preferir, 'to prefer, changes in the forms for I, you, he/she in the present tense as follows:

Prefiero el vino. I prefer wine.
Prefieres el agua. You prefer water. (*to friends*)
Prefiere el café. He/she prefers coffee.
Usted prefiere la cerveza. You prefer beer.

La vida española

Tragically, mugging is not uncommon in large cities in Spain. You will notice that Spanish women prefer shoulder bags with robust handles and they carry the bag in front of them, clutched tightly.

Goods and services

Shopping for clothes

Vocabulario básico

la camisa	the shirt
la talla	the size
la manga	the sleeve
el escaparate	the shop window
¿de qué es?	what's it made of?
el algodón	cotton
me la quedo	I'll take it

Diálogo

Dependiente	Buenos días, señora. ¿Qué desea?
Mujer	Quisiera ver algunas camisas, por favor.
Dependiente	Muy bien. ¿Qué talla?
Mujer	Una treinta y ocho.
Dependiente	Y, ¿de qué color?
Mujer	Blanca o amarilla.
Dependiente	Y, ¿con manga corta o larga?
Mujer	Corta.
Dependiente	¿Ésta, por ejemplo?
Mujer	Hay una en el escaparate que me gusta mucho.
Dependiente	¿Dónde está en el escaparate?
Mujer	A la derecha.
Dependiente	Es ésta, ¿no?
Mujer	Sí. ¿De qué es?
Dependiente	Es de algodón.
Mujer	Y, ¿cuánto vale?
Dependiente	Vale tres mil pesetas, señora.
Mujer	Muy bien. Me la quedo.

Ejercicios

1 Match the names of the goods in the window of the second-hand shop, writing down the number of the object and the letter of the name. Be careful! The letters of the names have been scrambled!

(a) dairo

(b) diestov

(c) atelam

(d) funadab

(e) flogadasse

(f) stopaza

______ ______ ______ ______ ______ ______

Cross reference with units:

5

26

27

2 On the recording three people are choosing goods in a shop. Fill in the grid, showing what they bought, with what features, colour and price.

Goods	Features	Colour	Price
1.			
2.			
3.			

3 Answer the questions to buy a size 36 shirt in green cotton with long sleeves.

- Y, ¿de qué color?
- ¿De algodón o de seda?
- Y, ¿con manga larga o corta?

Lenguaje

To close a sale in a Spanish shop, you use one of four phrases, changing the word underlined.

Me <u>lo</u> quedo. I'll take it. (The purchase is masculine and singular.)
Me <u>la</u> quedo. I'll take it. (The purchase is feminine and singular.)
Me <u>los</u> quedo. I'll take them. (The purchase is masculine and plural.)
Me <u>las</u> quedo. I'll take them. (The purchase is feminine and plural.)

La vida española

Much of shopping for clothes in Spain is now self-service. You select the garments you wish to try on and look for the fitting room – **Los probadores**.

To know the price, look for **P.V.P.** (**Precio de venta al público** – 'Price of sale to the public') on the ticket.

If you find **I.V.A.** (**Impuesto sobre el valor añadido**) you are paying VAT.

Emergencies

Dealing with a road accident

Vocabulario básico

loco/a	mad
el faro	the headlight
roto/a	broken
el parachoques	the bumper
tener la culpa	to be to blame
la culpa	the blame
usted causó	you caused
deprisa	quickly
arreglar	to repair
el accidente	the accident
usted vio	you saw
la ventanilla	the car window
la compañía de seguros	the insurance company
la multa	the fine

Diálogo

Mujer	¿Está usted loco?
Hombre	No, soy inglés.
Mujer	¡Mire mi coche! El faro está roto y el parachoques también.
Hombre	Yo no tengo la culpa. Usted salió de esa calle muy deprisa.
Mujer	Pero usted va a pagar para arreglar mi coche, ¿no?
Hombre	No, señora. Usted causó el accidente y no yo.
Mujer	¡Yo!
Hombre	Mire. Aquel guardia vio el accidente.
Mujer	¿Cuál?
Hombre	Aquél. ¡Señor guardia! Usted vio el accidente, ¿verdad?

Ejercicios

1 Say what is wrong with each object portrayed below. For example:

El faro está roto.

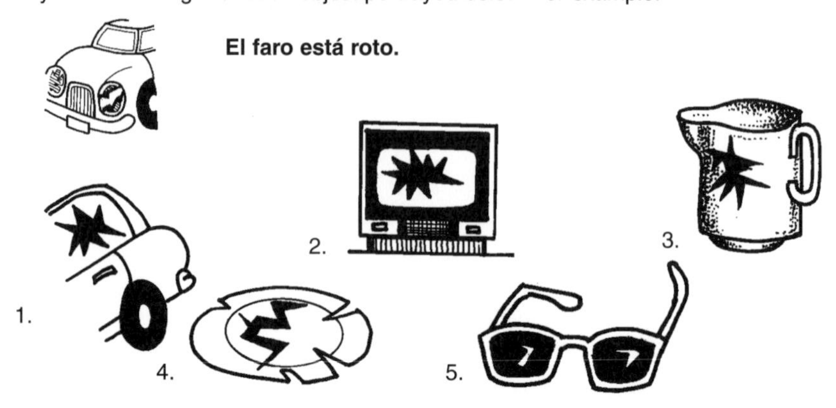

Cross reference with units:

43
46

2 What is broken? Read the following and say what is broken.

(a) ¡Mire mis gafas de sol!¡ Están rotas!
(b) ¡Mire! La lámpara está rota!
(c) ¡Caramba! La ventanilla del coche está rota.
(d) ¡Mire! El ordenador está roto y no funciona.

3 Recreate the dialogue on the facing page, using the following verbal cues to help you. (*Answers on page 132.*)

- Say no, you're French.
- Tell her it's not your fault. She came out of that street very fast.
- Say 'No, madam. You caused the accident, not me.'
- Say 'That gentleman saw the accident.'
- That one. Sir, you saw the accident, didn't you?'

Lenguaje

Roto (**rota**, **rotos**, **rotas**) describes a *state* which results from an *action*. Therefore it is used with **estar**.

El faro está roto.	The headlight is broken.
La ventanilla del coche está rota.	The car window is broken.
Los paneles están rotos.	The panels are broken.
Las puertas están rotas.	The doors are broken.

La vida española

Seat belts are compulsory in Spain when you are driving outside urban areas, but are *not* compulsory in towns., The maximum speed limits are:

60km/h – 37 mph in built-up areas
90 or 100 km/h – 56 or 62 mph on normal roads
100km/h – 62 mph on dual carriageways
120km/h – 75 mph on motorways.

You can be fined on the spot (**una multa**) by Spanish traffic police, and so it is best to obey the speed limits!

Unit 53 Food and drink

Making complaints in a restaurant

Vocabulario básico

el tenedor	the fork
el cuchillo	the knife
el vaso	the glass
perdone	forgive (me)
duro	stale (*of bread*), hard, difficult
pedir	to order (*food and drink*)
de marca	branded (*of wine*)
corriente	ordinary, plonk (*of wine*)
la molestia	the trouble

Diálogo

Cliente	¡Oiga, camarera!
Camarera	¿Señor?
Cliente	Este tenedor está sucio.
Camarera	Perdone, señor. Le traigo otro en seguida.
Cliente	El cuchillo de mi esposa está también sucio.
Camarera	Lo siento, señor. Lo cambio inmediatamente.
Cliente	Y el pan es duro.
Camarera	A ver. El camarero le trajo pan de ayer. ¿Algo más que no esté bien?
Cliente	Sí. Yo pedí vino de marca, pero éste es vino corriente.
Camarera	¿Qué marca pidió usted?
Cliente	Paternina Banda Azul.
Camarera	Lo voy a traer en seguida, y perdone la molestia.

Ejercicios

1 Make complaints about the following. For example:

Este tenedor está sucio.

1.

2.

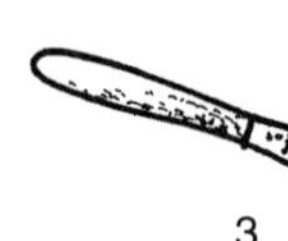

3.

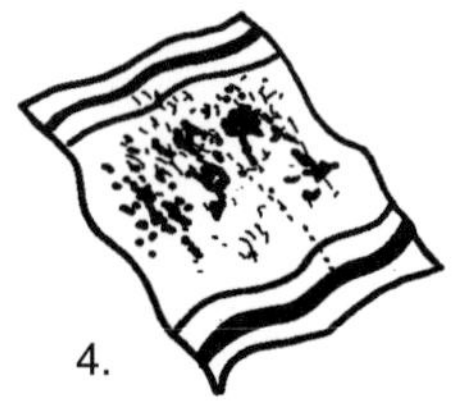

4.

5.

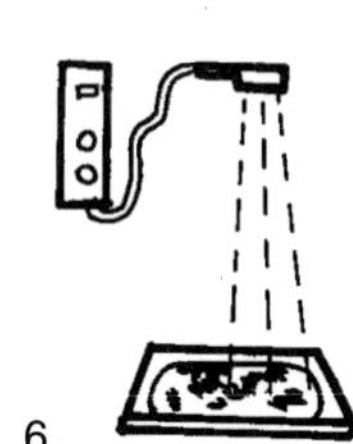

6.

Cross reference with units: 6 17 28 38

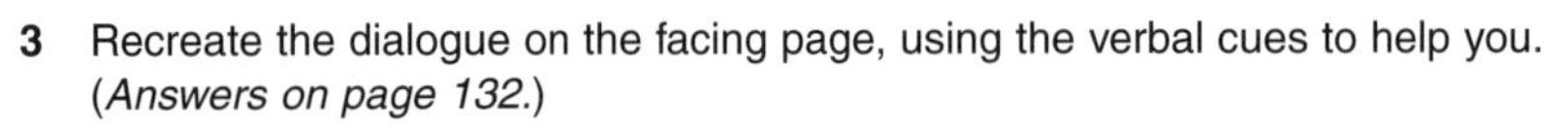

2 On the recording three people are making complaints in a restaurant. Fill in the grid to show the nature of the complaint and the remedy suggested.

Complaint	Remedy
1.	
2.	
3.	

3 Recreate the dialogue on the facing page, using the verbal cues to help you. (*Answers on page 132.*)

- Summon the waitress.
- Complain that this knife is dirty.
- Complain that your wife's/husband's glass is also dirty.
- Complain that the bread is hard.
- Say Yes, you ordered branded wine but this is ordinary wine.
- Say Rioja.

Lenguaje

The verb **pedir** is used to order food and drink. In the singular form of the present tense and in the 3rd person plural the **e** changes to **i**.

Pido vino.	I order wine.
Pides pan.	You order bread.
Pide cerveza.	He/She orders beer.
Usted pide agua.	You order water.

In the simple past, this change does *not* take place, but there is a change in the 3rd person singular and plural.

Pedí vino.	I ordered wine.
Pediste agua.	You ordered water.
Pidió vino de marca.	He/She ordered branded wine.
Usted pidió pan.	You ordered bread.
Pidieron pollo asado.	They ordered roast chicken.

La vida española

Waiters in Spain are thorough professionals, and manage to serve brilliantly without being either aggressive or servile. If you go to the same restaurant a few times and then miss a few days, when you return they will wish to know how they offended you. You have become part of the extended family which characterises many family-run restaurants.

UNIT 54 Travel

Travelling on the Madrid Metro

Vocabulario básico

el bonometro	a ticket for ten journeys
norteamericano/a	North American
especial	special
la manera	the way, the manner
permitir	to allow, to let
viajar	to travel
la red	the network, the net
la puerta	the door, the city gate
¿hay que cambiar?	Is it necessary to change? Must I change?
la dirección	the direction, the address
directo	direct

Diálogos

En la estación de Metro

Turista	Perdón, señor. ¿Qué es un bonometro exactamente?
Transeúnte	Usted no es de aquí, ¿verdad?
Turista	No, soy norteamericana.
Transeúnte	Pues, un bonometro es un billete especial.
Turista	¿Especial? ¿De qué manera?
Transeúnte	Le permite viajar por toda la red del Metro.
Turista	¿Por cuánto tiempo?
Transeúnte	Por diez viajes.
Turista	Gracias, señor.

En la estación de la Puerta del Sol

Turista	Perdón, señor. ¿Qué hago para llegar a la Plaza de Cibeles?
Viajero	Coja la dirección Ventas y baje en la segunda parada.
Turista	¿Hay que cambiar?
Viajero	No, señora, es directo.
Turista	Gracias, señor.

Ejercicios

1 Look at the line of the Metro system opposite. You are in the Puerta del Sol. Follow the instructions and write down which station you would arrive at.

1. Coja la dirección Miguel Hernández y baje en la tercera parada. __________
2. baje en la cuarta parada. ____________________
3. baje en la segunda parada. __________
4. baje en la quinta parada. ____________________

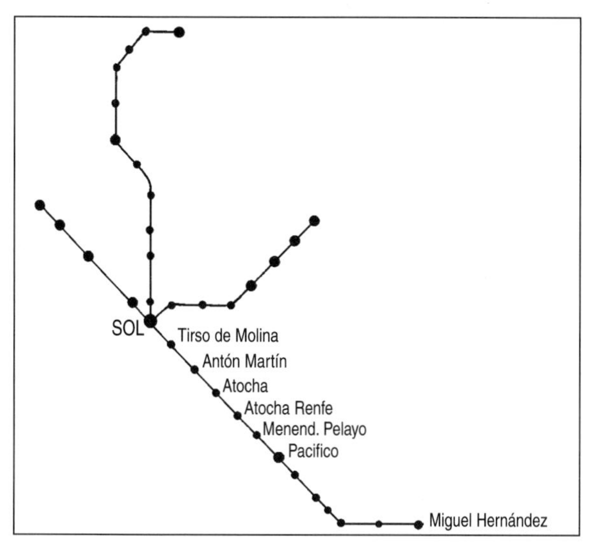

Cross reference with units:

2 On the recording three people are receiving directions. Fill in the grid to show where they should get off.

	Stop to alight at
1.	
2.	
3.	

3 Ask the Metro official:

1. What is a 'bonometro' exactly?
2. Explain that you are English.
3. Ask for how long.
4. Say thank you very much.

Lenguaje

Hay que + a verb allows you to express 'it is necessary', 'one should', etc.

Hay que visitar Sevilla.	One should visit Seville.
¿Hay que cambiar?	Is it necessary to change?

Americano/a normally means 'South American' to Spaniards because of their close cultural links to South America. **Norteamericano/a** is used to refer to people from the USA and Canada.

La vida española

The Madrid Metro system is a good way to get about the city. Two special tickets are available: the **bonometro**, which allows you to travel anywhere on the system for ten journeys, and the **carnet**, which allows ten journeys at a discount of 50 per cent. You select the line according to the name of the last station on it, and if you have to change you follow the sign **Correspondencia**.

Making plans

Arranging to go to a football match

Vocabulario básico

¿qué vas a hacer?	what are you going to do?
soler	to usually do something
suelo ir a misa	I usually go to Mass
a partir de	from (*time or price*)
el equipo	the team
la liga	the league
el estadio	the stadium
va a ser	it's going to be
estupendo	marvellous
el/la tenista	the tennis player

Diálogo

Pedro ¿Qué vas a hacer el domingo que viene, María?
María Suelo ir a misa por la mañana.
Pedro Y, ¿por la tarde?
María Pues, estoy libre a partir de la una.
Pedro ¿Por qué no vamos al partido?
María ¿Qué partido?
Pedro ¡Hombre! El partido de fútbol entre el Real Madrid y el Atlético de Bilbao.
María ¿Va a ser interesante?
Pedro Va a ser estupendo. Son los mejores equipos de la liga.
María Entonces, sí, me gustaría mucho. ¿Dónde nos vemos?
Pedro Delante del estadio a las dos y media. ¿Vale?
María Vale.

Ejercicios

1 Say what you usually do or don't do.
For example: **¿Fuma usted? ✘ No, no suelo fumar.**

1. **¿Sale usted en bicicleta?** ✓
2. **¿Come usted mucho?** ✓
3. **¿Practica usted el tenis?** ✓
4. **¿Da usted un paseo por el campo?** ✘
5. **¿Va usted a la piscina?** ✓

Cross reference with units:

2 On the recording three people are arranging an outing. Fill in the grid to show what they say.

Normal activity	Time when free	Idea accepted or reason why not
1.		
2.		
3.		

3 Recreate the dialogue on the facing page, using the verbal cues to help you. (*Answers on page 132.*)

- Say 'I usually work in the garden in the morning.'
- Say 'Well, I'm free from 3 o'clock.'
- Ask 'Which match?'
- Ask 'Is it going to be interesting?'
- Say 'Then I'd like to very much.' Ask 'Where shall we meet?'
- Say 'OK.'

Lenguaje

The verb **soler** allows you to express *elegantly* what you usually do or do not do. The present tense singular is as follows:

Suelo trabajar mucho.	I usually work a lot.
Sueles llegar tarde.	You usually arrive late.
Suele comer bien.	He/She usually eats well.
Usted suele jugar al golf los domingos.	You usually play golf on Sundays.

If you do not like to drink very much, you can escape from the hospitality of your Spanish friends with: **Gracias, no suelo beber mucho.** 'Thank you, I don't normally drink very much.'

La vida española

Bullfighting may be the national sport of Spain (and those who object to the 'sport' should remember that it is only foreign tourists who keep the activity economically viable), but football attracts the most supporters. Games are normally played on Sundays.

UNIT 56

Travel

Obtaining service in a petrol station

Vocabulario básico

la estación de servicio	the service station
el litro	the litre
la gasolina	the petrol
súper	4-star petrol
normal	3-star petrol
sin plomo	unleaded
el aceite	the oil (*most senses*)
está bien	it's fine
comprobar	to check
el neumático	the tyre

Diálogo

Empleado	Buenos días, señorita. ¿Qué le pongo?
Turista	Treinta litros de gasolina.
Empleado	¿Súper, normal o sin plomo?
Turista	Sin plomo, por favor.
Empleado	Ya está. ¿Algo más?
Turista	¿Quiere mirar el aceite?
Empleado	El aceite está bien. ¿Algo más?
Turista	¿Quiere comprobar los neumáticos?
Empleado	Los neumáticos están bien.
Turista	¿Qué le debo?
Empleado	Son tres mil seiscientas pesetas, señorita.

Ejercicios

1 Unscramble the word set in **bold** using the sense of the sentence to help you. All the words have to do with motoring.

(a) Adiós, señor, y buen **ajive**. __________

(b) ¿Es ésta la **tracerare** para Sevilla? __________

(c) ¿Se puede **crarapa** en esta calle? __________

(d) Quiero **laqurali** un coche, por favor. __________

2 On the recording two customers are making purchases at a service station. Mark the following statements TRUE or FALSE and try to correct the false ones.

1. She asks for 20 litres of 4-star and pays 2,400 pesetas. She also asks for cold drinks. __________
2. She buys 25 litres of unleaded and pays 3,000 pesetas. __________

Cross reference with units:

7 18 20 24 29 39 54

3 Recreate the dialogue on the facing page, using the following cues to help you. (*Answers on page 132.*)

- Ask for 40 litres of petrol.
- You want 4-star, please.
- Ask him to look at the water.
- Ask him to check the tyres.
- Ask how much you owe him.

Lenguaje

The word for 'oil' in most senses is **el aceite**. For your car, you simply ask for **aceite**.
¿Quiere poner un litro de aceite? 'Will you put a litre of oil in?'

For cooking, you ask for **aceite de oliva**, 'olive oil'.
¿Quiere darme un litro de aceite de oliva? 'Will you give me a litre of olive oil?'

To ask for something to be checked, you use **comprobar**.
¿Quiere comprobar la cuenta? 'Will you check the bill?'

La vida española

Petrol can be purchased by the litre – **Treinta litros, por favor**; or by the quantity of money – **Mil pesetas, por favor**; or by simply saying **Lleno**, 'Fill it up'. **La estación de servicio**, 'the service station', will normally provide the full range of services needed by a motorist; **la gasolinera**, 'the petrol station', will offer for sale petrol and oil and **el garaje**, 'the garage', is for parking only.

Talking about the past

Saying what the weather was like

Vocabulario básico

¿lo pasó usted bien?	did you enjoy yourself?
lo pasé muy bien	I enjoyed myself a lot
¿qué tiempo hacía?	what was the weather like?
hacía sol	it was sunny
hacía mucho calor	it was very hot
más de 30 grados	more than 30 degrees
tanto/a	so much
era	it was
climatizado	air-conditioned
podía	I was able

Diálogo

Mujer	¿Lo pasó usted bien en Mérida?
Hombre	Sí, lo pasé muy bien.
Mujer	¿Qué tiempo hacía?
Hombre	Hacía sol por la mañana.
Mujer	Y, ¿por la tarde?
Hombre	Hacía mucho calor. Más de treinta grados.
Mujer	Pero no podía dormir bien con tanto calor, ¿verdad?
Hombre	Por la noche hacía menos calor.
Mujer	Y era un hotel climatizado, ¿no?
Hombre	Sí, en el hotel todo era más cómodo.
Mujer	¿Piensa volver a Mérida?
Hombre	No, es una ciudad bastante pequeña.

Ejercicios

1 Look at the table and say aloud what the temperature was in the various locations. For example: **En los Pirineos la temperatura era de veinte grados.**

Pirineos	20
Málaga	31
Madrid	33
Valencia	25
Granada	28
Santander	22

Cross reference with units: 41 48

2 On the recording three people are discussing a visit and the weather. Fill in the grid below to indicate what they did.

Place visited	Did they enjoy the visit?	Weather
1.		
2.		
3.		

3 Look at the table given with Ejercicio 1, and answer the following questions:

1. ¿Hacía mucho calor en Madrid?
2. ¿Dónde hacia más calor, en Madrid o en Santander?
3. Hacía más calor en los Pirineos que en Granada?
4. Hacia más de treinta grados en Valencia?

Lenguaje

To indicate that you enjoyed yourself, you use the verb **pasar** in the past tense with the additional word **lo**, which is a pronoun meaning 'it' and refers to time.

Lo pasé muy bien. I enjoyed myself. (*Literally,* I spent it (time) very well.)

To say what the weather *was* like, the verb **hace** changes to **hacía**.

Hacía buen tiempo.	The weather was fine.
Hacía mal tiempo.	The weather was bad.
Hacía frío.	It was cold.
Hacía viento.	It was windy.

La vida española

In the summer in Spain, air-conditioning becomes vital. Public buildings such as cinemas and theatres indicate air-conditioning with the words **Local climatizado**, 'air-conditioned premises'. Hotels use a symbol of an air-conditioner and the words **Con aire acondicionado** in their publicity literature.

Emergencies

Reporting a mugging

Vocabulario básico

el ladrón	the thief
subió	he got on, in
la moto	the motorcycle
se fue	he went away
era	he was
tenía	he had
llevaba	he was wearing
la chaqueta	the jacket
los pantalones	the trousers
la camiseta	the tee-shirt

Diálogo

Mujer	¡Señor guardia!
Guardia	¿Señora? ¿Qué ocurre?
Mujer	Un ladrón me robó.
Guardia	¿Dónde?
Mujer	Aquí en la calle.
Guardia	¿Qué robó?
Mujer	Cogió mi bolso, subió a una moto y se fue por la calle.
Guardia	¿Cómo era el ladrón?
Mujer	Era muy alto y tenía unos veinte años.
Guardia	¿Qué llevaba?
Mujer	Llevaba una chaqueta de piel negra y pantalones grises.
Guardia	Vamos a la comisaría, señora. Ahí tienen muchas fotos de los ladrones que roban por la calles.

Ejercicios

1 **¿Qué robó?** Match the names to the objects, writing down the number of the object and the letter of the name.

1.

2.

3.

4.
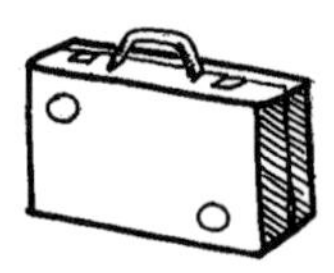

5.

6.
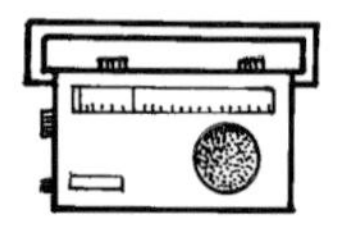

(a) **La radio** (b) **El dinero** (c) **La maleta** (d) **El pasaporte** (e) **Las gafas de sol** (f) **Los cheques de viaje**

________ ________ ________ ________ ________ ________

Cross reference with units: 11 22 43 46 52

2 On the recording two people are reporting a theft to the police. Fill in the grid below, giving the object stolen, where, and the appearance of the thief.

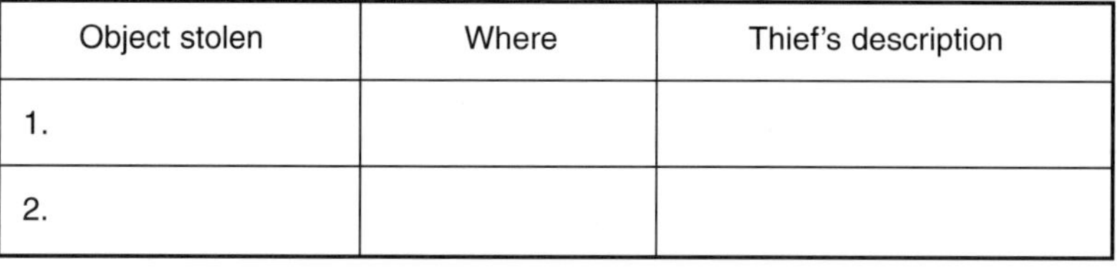

Object stolen	Where	Thief's description
1.		
2.		

3 Recreate the dialogue on the facing page, using the verbal cues to help you. (*Answers on page 132.*)

- Attract the policeman's attention.
- Say 'A thief robbed me.'
- Say 'Here on the square.'
- Say 'He grabbed my suitcase, got into a car and went away across the square.'
- Say he was very short and was about 25 years old.
- Say he was wearing a white t-shirt and grey trousers.

Lenguaje

To describe someone or say that something was going on in the past, you use the following tense, known as the imperfect.

Verbs ending in **-ar**

Llevaba una chaqueta negra.	I was wearing a black jacket.
Llevabas gafas de sol.	You were wearing sunglasses.
Llevaba pantalones grises.	He/She was wearing grey trousers.
Esperaba el autobús.	I was waiting for the bus.

Verbs ending in **-er** and **-ir**

Tenía unos veinte años.	I was about 20 years old.
Tenías más de diez años.	You were more than 10 years old.
Tenía unos treinta años.	He/She was about 30 years old.

La vida española

Theft from tourists is not uncommon in Spain, and precautions must be taken. A favourite technique is for two men on a motorbike to draw up alongside a car at traffic lights. Just before the lights change, they smash the window with a hammer, reach in, grab what they can and speed off just as the lights change. This happens in many major cities worldwide; but don't worry, it is unlikely to happen to you.

UNIT 59

Travel

Coping with a puncture

Vocabulario básico

el pinchazo	the puncture
encontrar	to find, to meet
el gato	the jack (*more commonly* the cat)
¿cómo es eso?	how is that?
alquilado	hired
el modelo	the model
el maletero	the boot, trunk (*American English*)
debajo de	underneath
la rueda de recambio	the spare wheel
el compañero	the companion

Diálogo

A traffic policeman stops to help a stranded motorist

Guardia	Buenas tardes, señora. ¿Qué ocurre?
Mujer	Tengo un pinchazo.
Guardia	Muy bien. Le voy a ayudar a cambiar la rueda.
Mujer	No puedo encontrar el gato.
Guardia	¿Cómo es eso?
Mujer	Es un coche alquilado.
Guardia	¡Ah! Ahora comprendo. Pues en ese modelo está en el maletero debajo de la rueda de recambio.
Mujer	Gracias.
Guardia	¿Tiene usted prisa?
Mujer	Sí, tengo que estar en el aeropuerto a las tres.
Guardia	No se preocupe. Mi compañero y yo vamos a cambiar la rueda en seguida.
Mujer	Muchísimas gracias. Son ustedes muy amables.

Ejercicios

1 You have met many people in this book. Can you write down in Spanish the words for the following people?

1. Female school pupil ______________________
2. Housewife ______________________
3. Architect ______________________
4. Waiter ______________________
5. Bus driver ______________________
6. Dentist ______________________
7. Student ______________________
8. Chemist ______________________
9. Policeman ______________________
10. Tourist ______________________

Cross reference with units: 7 18 20 24 29 39 54 56

2 On the recording three people are having problems with their car. Fill in the grid to show what the problem is.

Problem	Destination	Time they must arrive
1.		
2.		
3.		

3 Recreate the dialogue on the facing page, using the verbal cues to help you. (*Answers on page 133.*)

- Say 'I've got a puncture.'
- Say 'I can't find the jack.'
- Say 'It's my friend's car.'
- Say 'Thank you.'
- Say 'Yes, I've got to be in the Hotel Sol at 6.00.'
- Say 'Thank you very much. You are very kind.'

Lenguaje

The plural form of **usted** is **ustedes** and takes the same form as you use for 'they' – the 3rd person plural of the verb.

Ustedes son muy amables.	You are very kind.
Ustedes hablan muy bien el español.	You speak Spanish very well.
Ustedes viven en Madrid.	You live in Madrid.

Usted can be written in a short form, **Vd.**, and **ustedes** can be shortened to **Vds.**

La vida española

The Guardia Civil, feared and even hated under Franco, have now lost their bad reputation, and patrol the roads between towns helping motorists and controlling the traffic. When on foot patrol in town, they wear the distinctive **sombrero de tres picos** (three-cornered hat) made famous in the novel **El sombrero de tres picos**, by Antonio de Alarcón (1875) and the ballet by Manuel de Falla (1919).

UNIT 60 Travel

Saying goodbye at the airport

Vocabulario básico

entre nosotros	among us
el país	the country
fantástico	fantastic
Líneas Aéreas Iberia	Iberian Airlines
anuncia	announces
el destino	the destination
gracias por todo	thanks for everything
recuerdos a ...	regards to ...

Diálogo

Mujer	¿A qué hora sale el vuelo para Londres?
Hombre	Sale a las once y media.
Mujer	¿Lo pasaste bien entre nosotros?
Hombre	Lo pasé bomba. Las mejores vacaciones de mi vida.
Mujer	Y, ¿qué piensas de España ahora?
Hombre	Es un país fantástico, y la gente es muy simpática.
Altavoz	Líneas Aéreas Iberia anuncia la salida de su vuelo, número 325, destino Londres. Todos los pasajeros a la puerta 15, por favor.
Hombre	Es mi vuelo. Gracias, por todo, María.
Mujer	Recuerdos a la familia. ¿Qué vas a hacer durante el vuelo?
Hombre	Voy a estudiar más el español.
Mujer	Adiós, y hasta el año que viene.
Hombre	Adiós.

Ejercicios

1 Which is the 'odd one out' in these short lists.

(a) Vino tinto; vino blanco; agua verde.
(b) Agua mineral con gas; agua mineral con cerveza; agua mineral sin gas.
(c) Un partido de teatro; un partido de golf; un partido de tenis.
(d) Ensalada mixta; helado de queso; sopa de pescado.
(e) Hace mucho sol; hace blanco; hace viento.

2 On the recording three flight announcements are made. Mark the following statements TRUE or FALSE, and correct the false ones.

1. Iberia announce flight No. 125 to New York. Passengers should go to Gate 21.
2. British Air announce flight No. 312 to Paris. Passengers should proceed to Gate 14.

3. Air France announce flight No. 126 to Chicago.
   Passengers should go to Gate 28.

3 Travel questions. What are the questions to obtain the following information? (*Answers on page 133.*)

(a) At what time does the flight leave for London?
(b) At what time does the bus leave for the city centre?
(c) At what time does the taxi leave for the theatre?
(d) At what time does the train leave for Toledo?

Lenguaje

Lo pasé bomba, 'I had a splendid time', is a colloquial expression which will convince people that you have been studying Spanish for years!

Recuerdos a + family or person's name, allows you to send best regards to people.

Recuerdos a tu madre. Best regards to your mother.
Recuerdos a tus hijos. Best wishes to your children.

This expression can be used in speech or writing.

La vida española

You have now learned some very useful, basic Spanish which will enable you to cope with many everyday situations in Spain and Latin America.

Many congratulations on finishing the course!

Cross reference with units: 7 18 20 24 29 39 54 56 59

Answers to exercises

UNIT 1 **1** 1. Soy la señora Gómez. Soy de Valencia. 2. Soy la señorita Blanco. Soy de Madrid. 3. Soy el señor Amodia. Soy de Sevilla. **2** 1. Señor Sala. Madrid. 2. Señora Blanco. Málaga. 3. Señorita Pérez. Not given. **3** Soy el señor/la señoras.la señorita + surname. • Sí, soy inglés/inglesa. • Soy de + name of town.

UNIT 2 **1** 1. d 2. a 3. f 4. e 5. c 6. b. **2** 1. Losada. Single room. Shower. 5 nights. Room 6. 2. Pérez. Double room. Bath. 6 nights. Room 4. **3** (a) Una habitación individual con baño para tres días. (b) Una habitación doble con ducha para dos días. (c) Una habitación individual con ducha para seis días.

UNIT 3 **1** 1. (1b); 2. (5c); 3. (4d) **2** 1. Sagunto. East, near Valencia. Roman theatre. 2. Sevilla. South. Impressive cathedral. **3** • Soy de + town name. • Está en + country name. • Es grande/bastante grande/pequeña/ bastante pequeña. • Hay una catedral/ hay un museo/no hay nada.

UNIT 4 **1** 1. Mercado municipal. 2. Banco Central. 3. Hotel Breton. **2** 1. Hotel España – Along the street, second on the left. The hotel is in that street beside the Goya Cinema. 2. A bank – The Banco Popular is at the end of the street on the left. It is not far. **3** • ¿Por dónde se va al Banco Central? • ¿Está lejos? • Y, ¿está abierto ahora?

UNIT 5 **1** (a) Dos y dos son cuatro. (b) Tres y dos son cinco. (c) Cuatro y dos son seis. (d) Tres y cuatro son siete. (e) Cinco y tres son ocho. **2** 1. Dollars. 30. Cash desk 5. 2. Pounds sterling. 40. Cash desk 8. **3** • Quiero cambiar unos cheques de viaje, por favor. • Quiero cambiar cuarenta dólares. • Aquí tiene usted mi pasaporte.

UNIT 6 **1** 1. c 2. b 3. e 4. a 5. d. **2** (a) A black coffee (b) A beer and a cheese sandwich (c) A white coffee and a bun. **3** • Un café con leche. • ¿Qué tiene para comer? • Un sandwich de jamón y tomate. • Eso es.

UNIT 7 **1** (a) Un billete de ida y vuelta, segunda clase para Toledo. (b) Un billete de ida, segunda clase para Madrid. (c) Un billete de ida y vuelta, primera clase para Málaga. (d) Un billete de ida, primera clase para Córdoba. **2** 1. 2 tickets. Second class, return, to Sevilla. 2. 3 tickets. First class, single, to Málaga. 3. 1 ticket. Second class, return, to Valencia. **3** • ¿A qué hora sale el próximo tren para Barcelona? • Dos billetes, por favor. • De ida. • De primera. • ¿De dónde sale el tren?

UNIT 8 **1** 1. b 2. c 3. d 4. a **2** 1. Golf 2. Tennis 3. Football 4. Keen on books. **3** • Practico el fútbol. • ¿Practica usted algún deporte? • Sí, practica el tenis en el colegio. • También es aficionado a los libros.

UNIT 9 **1** 1. b 2. d 3. a 4. e 5. c **2** 1. Madrid – sunny and very hot. 2. Pyrenees – very bad weather. 3. Seville – very fine weather and very sunny. 4. N. Spain – bad weather; very cold. **3** • Hace sol. • Hace frío. • Hace calor. • Hace mal tiempo.

UNIT 10 **1** 8 ocho; 26 veintiséis; 35 treinta y cinco; 42 cuarenta y dos; 83 ochenta y tres; 58 cincuenta y ocho; 74 setenta y cuatro; 12 doce; 9 nueve; 97 noventa y siete; 61 sesenta y uno; 123 ciento veintitrés. **2** 1. a 2. c 3. b. **3** a) Cuarenta y cinco y cincuenta y cinco son cien. b) Veintiuno y doce son treinta y tres c) Sesenta y cuatro y veintidós son ochenta y seis d) Treinta y cinco y treinta y ocho sen setenta y tres. e) Cincuenta y dos y diecisiete son sesenta y nueve.

UNIT 11

1 2. d 3. c 4. a 5. b. Missing caption: 1. Un bolso. **2** 1. Handbag. Quite big. Colour not given. Leather. English money, English passport, sunglasses. 2. Handbag. Size not given. Green. Fabric not given. Traveller's cheques, passport. 3. Bag. Size not given. Blue. Plastic. Credit cards, sunglasses, scarf. **3** 1. Es pequeño. 2. En verde. 3. Es de piel.

UNIT 12

1 Manolo tiene diez años. Juan tiene cuarenta años. Pepe tiene cuatro años. Marta tiene siete años. Pablo tiene treinta años. **2** 1. Married. 1 Child. José. 21. Student. 2. Married. 2 Children. Marta; Pepa. 7 and 5. Schoolchildren. **3** a) Tengo un hijo; Se llama Manuel; tiene veinte años y es estudiante en la universidad. b) Tengo dos hijos; un hijo y una hija. Se llaman Pepe y Marta y tienen dieciocho y veintidós años.

UNIT 13

1 1. La habitación vale ocho mil pesetas. 2. El desayuno vale trescientas pesetas. 3. La comida vale dos mil pesetas. 4. La cena vale dos mil trescientas pesetas. **2** a) ¿Individual o doble? b) ¿Para cuántos dias? c) ¿Con baño o con ducha? d) Cuánto vale la habitación? **3** • ¿Tiene una habitación libre? • Doble, por favor. • Para cinco días, hasta el viernes. • ¿Cuánto vale la habitación? • ¿Cuánto valen las comidas? • Gracias.

UNIT 14

1 Plasencia está cerca de Cáceres. Carmona está cerca de Sevilla. Chinchón está cerca de Mádrid. Sabadell está cerca de Barcelona. **2** 1. Near Sevilla. Tourist town. Very pleasant people. 2. Near Madrid. Village; 4,000 inhabitants. Quite pleasant people. 3. Near Barcelona. Industrial town. Very pleasant people. **3** Está cerca de Madrid. Tiene cuatro mil habitantes. La catedral es muy bonita. La gente es muy simpática.

UNIT 15

1 1. c 2. d 3. a 4. e 5. b **2** 1. Chemist's – Straight ahead, turn right, first left. 2. Bank – Straight ahead, turn right, go to the end of the street. **3** • Perdón. ¿Hay un banco en esta parte de la ciudad? • ¿Por dónde se va a la Plaza Mayor? • Sí. • Gracias.

UNIT 16

1 The shopper forgot to buy ¼ kilo of ham, and crisps. **2** 1. False. She bought ½ kilo of cheese. 2. True. **3** *En la charcutería* • Póngame medio kilo de jamón. • Sí, un kilo de queso. • Sí. ¿Cuánto es todo? *En la verdulería.* • Póngame dos lechugas y un kilo de tomates. *En el puesto de comestibles.* • Déme cuatro panecillos y una botella de agua mineral. • Sin gas.

UNIT 17

1 1. Crema de espárragos 2. Ensalada mixta 3. Tortilla española 4. Chuleta de cerdo 5. Vino blanco. **2** 1. Cold soup; pork chop without chips; fizzy mineral water. 2. Asparagus soup; Spanish omelette; half bottle of house white wine. **3** • Tráigame una crema de espárragos. • Voy a tomar la chuleta de cerdo. • Sí, con patatas. • Sí, una botella de vino blanco. • Sí, un helado.

UNIT 18

1 (a) ¿A qué hora sale el próximo tren para Madrid? (b) Un billete de ida y vuelta. (c) ¿De dónde sale el tren? **2** *Dialogue 1*: 1. False. 2. True. He wants the Barcelona train. 3. True. *Dialogue 2*: 1. True. 2. False. It is going to Valencia. 3. True. *Dialogue 3*: 1. True. 2. False. She wants a cheap hotel. 3. True. **3** *En la estación* • ¿Es éste el tren para Valencia? • Entonces, ¿de dónde sale el tren para Valencia? *En el andén*

• Perdón, señor. ¿De dónde sale el tren para Valencia? • Gracias. *En el departamento* • Aquí tiene usted. ¿A qué hora llega el tren a Valencia? • ¿Conoce usted un buen hotel en Valencia?

UNIT 19

1 1. Cuando hace buen tiempo, practico el tenis. 2. Cuando hace mal tiempo, veo la televisión. 3. Cuando hace sol, tomo el sol. 4. Cuando hace frío, voy al cine. 5. Cuando hace frío, escucho un disco. **2** 1. Sunny weather. Man sunbathes in garden; woman sunbathes on beach. 2. Bad weather. Woman stays in, reads a novel or watches TV; man goes to the cinema or the theatre. 3. Cold weather. Man stays in and watches TV or works.
3 Cuando hace buen tiempo voy a la piscina/tomo el sol. Si hace mucho frío veo la televisión/me quedo en casa. Cuando hace mal tiempo me quedo en casa/veo la televisión. Si hace mucho sol voy a la piscina/tomo el sol.

UNIT 20

1 1. El Seat Ibiza vale cinco mil trescientas pesetas por día. 2. El Ford Escort vale seis mil quinientas pesetas por día. 3. El Fiat Tipo vale siete mil novecientas pesetas por día. 4. El Renault 21 vale doce mil seiscientas pesetas por día. 5. El Ford Fiesta vale cinco mil pesetas por día. **2** 1. Ford Escort; 6.500 pesetas; for 6 days. 2. Renault 5; 4.500 pesetas; for 4 days.
3 • Buenos días. Aquí puedo alquilar un coche, ¿verdad? • Un coche económico. • Un Renault 5 entonces. • Para dos días. Queremos visitar El Escorial.

UNIT 21

1 1. d 2. g 3. h 4. j 5. i 6. b 7. c 8. a 9. f 10. e. **2** 1. Sevilla; 16th-century cathedral. 2. Madrid; 19th-Century museum, El Prado. **3** castillo; interés; abierto; cara.

UNIT 22

1 1. ¿Tiene algo para el dolor de estómago? 2. ¿Tiene algo para el dolor de cabeza? 3. ¿Tiene algo para las quemaduras del sol? **2** 1. False. She has sunburn, but the cream costs 1,000 pesetas. 2. True. 3. False. She is given Okal but it costs 500 pesetas.
3 a) ¿Tiene algo para el dolor de cabeza? b) ¿Tiene algo para las quemaduras del sol? c) Déme un tubo. d) ¿Cuánto es todo?

UNIT 23

1 1. c 2. d 3. a 4. b. **2** All answers are correct. **3** • Sí, tengo dos: un hermano y una hermana. • Mi hermana es alta y delgada. Tiene el pelo muy largo. • Es bajo y gordo. Tiene el pelo corto. • Sí, es muy inteligente.

UNIT 24

1 1. Toledo está a cuatrocientos veintidós kilómetros de Vitoria. 2. Valencia está a seiscientos kilómetros de Zamora. 3. Toledo está a doscientos cincuenta y ocho kilómetros de Valladolid. 4. Zamora está a noventa y seis kilómetros de Valladolid.
2 1. Segovia. Road no. 110. 1 hour. 2. Madrid. Road no. 6. 1 ½ hours.
3 • Perdón. ¿Es ésta la carretera para Toledo? • ¿Qué tengo que hacer para llegar a Toledo? • Y, ¿cuánto se tarda en llegar a Toledo? • Gracias.

UNIT 25

1 Habitación; cuarto de baño; baño; cama; ducha; gafas de sol; novela; mesa; bufanda. Did you find any more? **2** 1. False. The Hotel Tilos is recommended, but the phone number is 31 80 98. 2. False. A room is available, but the price is 8,000 pesetas.
3 a) ¿Tiene una habitación libre? b) Para hoy. c) Lo siento. d) No tengo nada libre. e) ¿Tiene el número de teléfono de ese hotel? f) Muchas gracias.

UNIT 26

1 1. c 2. e 3. b 4. d 5. a.
2 a) ¿Tieno un plano de la ciudad? b) ¿Cuánto vale? c) ¿Qué hay para los turistas en Avila? **3** • Buenos días. ¿Tiene usted un plano de la ciudad?

• ¿Cuánto vale? • ¿Qué hay para los turistas en Sevilla? • ¿Puede darme un mapa de la región?

UNIT 27 **1** 1. La jarra grande vale novecientas pesetas. 2. La jarra pequeña vale quinientas pesetas. 3. El plato grande vale trescientas pesetas. 4. El plato pequeño vale mil pesetas.
2 1. True. 2. False. The price is 2.000 pesetas. 3. False. She wants a cheaper one and buys it for 1.000 pesetas.
3 a) Lo siento, no comprendo. ¿Qué es una jarra? b) Ah, sí. Ahora comprendo. c) Sí, pero, ¿tiene otra más grande? d) Sí. ¿Cuánto vale? e) Ésa, por favor.

UNIT 28 **1** (a) un bistec = a steak (b) patatas fritas = chips (c) una manzana = an apple (d) una pera = a pear (e) un plátano = a banana (f) fresas = strawberries. **2** 1. a 2. c 3. b
3 • ¿Qué tal el melón? • El melón entonces. • Pollo asado. • Sí, con patatas. • Una botella de vino blanco.

UNIT 29 **1** 1. El señor Pérez va a Córdoba. 2. La señora González va a Granada. 3. La señorita Losada va a Málaga. 4. El señor Amodia va a Bilbao.
2 1. The airport. Hurry not given. 2. The Main Square. No hurry. 3. The airport. No hurry. **3** a) Salidas, por favor. b) Internacionales, por favor. c) Voy a Londres.

UNIT 30 **1** (a) Juego al tenis en el jardín. (b) ¿Practica algún deporte? (c) Soy aficionada a las novelas. (d) ¿Qué hace usted en su tiempo libre?
2 1. Golf. Sports centre. Wife. 2. Swimming. Swimming-pool. Daughter. 3. Tennis. The garden. Children.
3 • No me gusta. Es muy aburrido. • Me gusta mucho el tenis. • No, con mi amiga Lola. • ¿Cuál es su pasatiempo favorito?

UNIT 31 **1** 1. Me gusta más el pescado. 2. Me gusta más el vino. 3. Me gusta más esquiar. 4. Me gusta más la fruta. 5. Me gusta más el tenis.
2 a) Nonsense. b) Sense. c) Nonsense. d) Nonsense. **3** • Me gusta dar un paseo por el campo. • Me gusta ver la televisión. • Me gustan más los programas de deportes.

UNIT 32 **1** 1. María empieza a las nueve y termina a las cinco. 2. Pedro empieza a las diez y termina a las siete. 3. Juan empieza a las doce y termina a las diez. 4. Lola empieza a las tres y termina a las siete. **2** a) ¿A qué hora se levanta usted? b) ¿A qué hora empieza su trabajo? c) ¿Cómo es el trabajo? d) ¿A qué hora termina por la tarde?
3 • Me levanto a las siete y media. • Me visto y tomo el desayuno. • No, cojo el autobús. • Empiezo a las nueve y cuarto.

UNIT 33 **1** 1. ¿Por qué no vamos al cine? 2. ¿Por qué no vamos a la piscina? 3. ¿Por qué no vamos al Museo del Prado? 4. ¿Por qué no vamos a la discoteca?
2 1. Sunday. To play tennis. In front of house. 11 a.m. 2. Friday. To go to cinema. In front of cinema. 7.00. **3** • Sí, creo que sí. • ¡Qué buena idea! • Delante del Café Sol. • A las dos de la tarde. ¿Vale?

UNIT 34 **1** El padre es bajo y gordo. La madre es alta y delgada. El hijo es alto con el pelo muy corto. La hija es baja y delgada. Los abuelos son altos y muy viejos. El tío es bajo y gordo. La tía es alta y delgada. **2** 1. Grandparents. Josefina; Juan. 80; 75. Characteristics not given. 2. Brother. Paco. 25. Quite intelligent. 3. Uncle; aunt. Alberto; Carmen. Ages not given. Very pleasant. **3** a) Quién es este hombre? b) Es bajo, ¿verdad? c) ¿Cuántos años tiene? d) ¿Es simpático? e) ¿Cómo se llama esta señora?

UNIT 35 **1** 1. c 2. e 3. d 4. a 5. f 6. b.
2 1. c 2. a 3. b. **3** • Me parece que esta sábana está sucia. • Y la televisión

no funciona. • Sí. La lámpara de la mesa no funciona.

UNIT 36 **1** 1. Sí, me gustaría. 2. Sí, me gustaría mucho. 3. No, no me gustaría. 4. Sí, me gustaría. **2** 1. Málaga. Tuesday. Cathedral; good shops. 2. Toledo. Sunday. Cathedral; several museums. **3** • Sí, me gustaría mucho. • ¿Es una ciudad interesante? • ¿Qué hay de interés? • ¿A qué hora quiere usted salir? • Adiós, hasta el domingo.

UNIT 37 **1** 1. Se venden en la frutería. 2. Se vende en la carnicería. 3. Se compran en Correos. 4. Se compra en la lechería. **2** 1. Records. Record shop. End of street, on the right. 2. Ham. Delicatessen. In the Main Square. 3. Bananas. Market. At the end of the street. **3** • ¿Cuánto valen las tarjetas postales? • Estas cinco, por favor. • Aquí tiene usted. ¿Los sellos se venden aquí? • ¿Por dónde se va a Correos?

UNIT 38 **1** 1. c 2. a 3. d 4. b. **2** 1. True. 2. False. He orders more red wine. **3** • ¡Camarera! • ¿Quiere traerme más patatas fritas? • Mi hijo tiene sed. Tráigame una botella de agua mineral. • Con gas. • Sí. Uvas para mí y un helado para mi hijo.

UNIT 39 **1** a) Catch the number 3 bus and get off at the fourth stop. b) Get off at the next stop, cross the street and there is the theatre. c) Catch the number 10 bus and get off in the Main Square. That's where the Central Bank is. **2** 1. The beach. Journey lasts about 10 minutes. 2. Toledo. Coach leaves at 10.30; arrives at 2 p.m.; ticket costs 800 pesetas. **3** a) ¿Es éste el autobús para la estación de ferrocarriles? b) ¿Cuál es el autobús para la estación de ferrocarriles? c) De dónde sale el autobús? d) Está cerca la estación de ferrocarriles?

UNIT 40 **1** 1. A Pepe le encanta el fútbol. 2. A Marta le encanta el tenis. 3. A Manuel le encanta el cine. 4. A Juana le encanta el teatro. **2** 1. Walks in country with husband. Watches TV if the weather is bad. 2. Visiting museums. Very exciting and fairly cheap. 3. Golf. Plays with her friend Isabel; plays quite well. **3** a) Cuál es tu pasatiempo favorito? b) ¿Dónde practicas el windsurf? c) ¿Sabes nadar? d) ¿Hablas algún idioma?

UNIT 41 **1** 1. María visitó Valencia y compró un bolso. 2. Rafael visitó Sevilla y compró un disco. 3. Carmen visitó Málaga y compró una jarra. 4. Pepe visitó Toledo y compró un libro. **2** a) ¿Dónde pasó usted el fin de semana? b) ¿Le gusto? c) ¿Sacó usted muchas fotos? d) ¿Compró usted algún recuerdo? e) ¿Costó mucho? **3** • Visité Madrid con mi amiga. • Sí, me gustó mucho. • Sí, saqué fotos del Museo del Prado. • Sí, compré este bolso. • No, sólo cinco mil pesetas.

UNIT 42 **1** 1. House in ruins. Entry forbidden. 2. Inflammable gas. Smoking prohibited. 3. Parking prohibited. Private garage. 4. Forbidden to sell tobacco to anyone under 16 years old. 5. Washing cars forbidden. Fine of 10,000 pesetas. **2** 1. Prohibited. 2. Prohibited. 3. Permitted. 4. Permitted. 5. Prohibited. 6. Visit the cathedral – permitted. **3** a) No, no se puede. b) Sí, se puede. c) No, no se puede. d) Sí, se puede/No, no se puede e) No, no se puede.

UNIT 43 **1** 1. El ladrón robó un pasaporte en un bolso en el coche. 2. El ladrón robó una maleta en una habitación en el hotel. 3. El ladrón robó un bolso en una mesa en el café **2** a) False b) True c) False d) False e) True. **3** • Quiero denunciar un robo. • Hace media hora. • En la habitación del hotel. • Un bolso. • Dinero, y mi pasaporte.

UNIT 44 **1** 1. Fui a la farmacia y compré unas aspirinas. 2. Fui a la zapatería y compré unos zapatos. 3. Fui a la charcutería y compré medio kilo de queso. **2** 1. Last Saturday. Main Square. Sunglasses at 2,000 pesetas. 2. Last Friday. Montera St. Shoes at 10,000 pesetas. 3. Last Wednesday. Main St. Scarf at 5,500 pesetas. **3** a) Fuiste de compras la semana pasada? b) ¿Dónde está esa tienda? c) ¿Compraste algo? d) ¿Te costó mucho? e) Una ganga, ¿no?

UNIT 45 **1** 1. El abuelo se llama Alonso. La abuela se llama Pilar. El padre se llama Pedro. La madre se llama María. El nieto se llama Paco. La nieta se llama Marta. 2. El abuelo tiene sesenta y cinco años. La abuela tiene sesenta y dos años. El padre tiene treinta y siete años. La madre tiene treinta y cinco años. El nieto tiene once años. La nieta tiene diez años. 3. La abuela es ama de casa. El abuelo está jubilado. La madre es jefa de marketing. El padre es dentista. **2** 1. False. She is single and works as an English teacher. 2. False. He has one daughter who is a policewoman. 3. True. **3** 1. está. 2. es. 3. está. 4. está. 5. es.

UNIT 46 **1** head, **la cabeza**; stomach, **el estómago**; throat, **la garganta**; tooth, **la muela**; eye, **el ojo**; hand, **la mano**; foot, **el pie**; arm, **el brazo**; leg, **la pierna**; ear, **la oreja**; mouth, **la boca**. **2** 1. Stomach and throat. 2. Feet and hand. 3. Tooth. **3** • Me duele mucho la cabeza. • Me duele la garganta. • Cuatro horas. • Sí, más de treinta grados. ¿Es grave? • ¿Qué tengo que hacer?

UNIT 47 **1** (a) ¿Cuántos años tiene usted? (b) ¿De qué color es? (c) ¿A qué hora sale el tren? (d) ¿Cuántos alumnos hay en la clase? (e) ¿Cómo se llama usted? **2** 1. Room 25. Comedor. Dining-room. Credit card. 2. Room 33. IVA. VAT. Eurocheque. 3. Room 110. Llamadas internacionales. Phone bill. Cash. **3** 1. Fond of sleeping. 2. Greedy, a big eater. 3. Talkative 4. Hard-drinker.

UNIT 48 **1** 1. c 2. d 3. e 4. a 5. b. **2** a) More than 100 million pesetas. b) More than 20 million pesetas. c) The new novels. **3** • Muy bien. Fui a la Feria de la Piel. • Sí, recibí muchos pedidos para los nuevos zapatos. • Sí, mucho. Más de cincuenta pedidos. • Sí. En total más de treinta millones de pesetas.

UNIT 49 **1** 1. Dining-room, **el comedor**; table, **la mesa**; chairs, **las sillas**. 2. Kitchen, cooker, **la cocina**; fridge, **la nevera**; dishwasher, **el lavaplatos**. 3. Bathroom, **el cuarto de baño**; bath, **el baño**; shower, **la ducha**. 4. Living room, **el salón**; sofa, **el sofá**; armchairs, **las butacas**; TV, **la televisión**. 5. Bedroom, **el dormitorio**; bed, **la cama**; wardrobe, **el armario**. **2** 1. 2 bedrooms. Gas cooker; fridge; table in kitchen. Sofa, armchair, radio in living room. 2. 6 bedrooms. Electric cooker, fridge, dishwasher, table in kitchen. 2 sofas, 3 armchairs, radio, TV in living room. 3. 4 bedrooms. Fridge, dishwasher, gas cooker, table and 4 chairs in kitchen. Sofa, 3 armchairs, TV in living room. **3** 1. Nonsense. 2. Nonsense. 3. Sensible. 4. Nonsense. 5. Nonsense.

UNIT 50 **1** (a) tren (b) estación (c) autobús (d) billete (e) andén. **2** 1. Hotel Plaza. Plaza de España, 1 km. Metro advised. Prefers bus. 2. Museo del Prado. Very far. Advised to catch bus. Taxi more comfortable. **3** • ¿Puede ayudarme? Estoy perdida. • Busco el Hotel Atlántico en la calle del Arenal. • ¿Qué hago? Tengo una cita en el hotel a las cinco. • No, prefiero coger un taxi. • Ahí viene uno. ¡Taxi! ¡Taxi!

UNIT 51 **1** 1. e 2. c 3. f 4. b 5. d 6. a.

2 1. Shirts. Size 41, long sleeves. Green. 5,000 pesetas. 2. Shirt. Size 38, short sleeves, cotton. Blue. 6,000 pesetas. 3. Shirt. Size 40, short sleeves. White. 7,000 pesetas. **3** Una treinta y seis. Verde. De algodón. Larga.

UNIT 52

1 1. La ventanilla está rota. 2. La televisión está rota. 3. La jarra está rota. 4. El plato está roto. 5. Las gafas de sol están rotas. **2** a) Sunglasses. b) Lamp. c) Car window. d) Computer. **3** • No, soy francés. • Yo no tengo la culpa. Usted salió de esa calle muy de prisa. • No, señora. Usted causó el accidente y yo no. • Aquel señor vio el accidente. • Aquél. Señor, usted vio el accidente, ¿verdad?

UNIT 53

1 1. Este vaso está sucio. 2. Este plato está sucio. 3. Este cuchillo está sucio. 4. Esta sábana está sucia. 5. Este baño está sucio. 6. Esta ducha está sucia. **2** 1. Fizzy mineral water instead of still. Another bottle brought. 2. Dirty glass. Clean glass brought. 3. White wine for red wine. Red wine brought immediately. **3** • Camarera. • Este cuchillo está sucio. • El vaso de mi esposa/esposo está sucio también. • El pan es duro. • Sí. Yo pedí vino de marca, pero éste es vino corriente. • Rioja.

UNIT 54

1 1. Atocha. 2. Atocha Renfe. 3. Antón Martín. 4. Menéndez Pelayo. **2** 1. Portazgo; 3rd stop. 2. Plaza de Castilla; 1st stop. 3. Ventas; 5th stop. **3** 1. ¿Qué es un bonometro exactamente? 2. Soy inglés (inglesa). 3. ¿Por cuánto tiempo? 4. Muchas gracias.

UNIT 55

1 1. Sí, suelo salir en bicicleta. 2. Sí, suelo comer mucho. 3. Sí, suelo practicar el tenis. 4. No, no suelo dar un paseo por el campo. 5. Sí, suelo ir a la piscina. **2** 1. Work in garden. Free at 2 p.m. He doesn't like shopping. 2. Visit mother. Free at 3 p.m. They agree to go swimming if the weather is fine. 3. Work until 5.00. Free at 7.00. He cannot understand French films. **3** • Suelo trabajar en el jardín por la mañana. • Pues estoy libre a partir de las tres. • ¿Qué partido? • ¿Va a ser interesante? • Entonces me gustaría mucho. ¿Dónde nos vemos? • Vale.

UNIT 56

1 (a) viaje (b) carretera (c) aparcar (d) alquilar. **2** 1. True. 2. False. She buys 30 litres of two-star and pays 3,000 pesetas. **3** • Cuarenta litros de gasolina. • Súper, por favor. • ¿Quiere mirar el agua? • ¿Quiere comprobar los neumáticos? • ¿Qué le debo?

UNIT 57

1 En Málaga la temperatura era de treinta y un grados. En Madrid la temperatura era de treinta y tres grados. En Valencia la temperatura era de veinticinco grados. En Granada la temperatura era de veintiocho grados. En Santander la temperatura era de veintidós grados. **2** 1. Málaga. Yes. Fine, 32 degrees. 2. Madrid. Not at all. Too hot. 3. The Pyrenees. Yes; could ski every day. Very cold. **3** 1. Si. (Hacía mucho calor). 2. Hacía más calor en Madrid. 3. No, no, hacía más calor en los Pirineos que en Granada. 4. No, hacía veinticinco grados en Valencia.

UNIT 58

1 1. f 2. b 3. e 4. c 5. d 6. a. **2** 1. Suitcase. Hotel car-park. Very thin, 15 years old, white t-shirt, black trousers. 2. Money. Bank doorway. Quite short and fat, 30 years old, brown jacket, green trousers. **3** • ¡Señor guardia! • Un ladrón me robó. • Aquí en la plaza. • Cogió mi maleta, subió a un coche y se fue por la plaza. • Era muy bajo y tenía unos veinticinco años. • Llevaba una camiseta blanca y pantalones grises.

UNIT 59

1 1. La alumna 2. El ama de

casa 3. El arquitecto 4. El camarero 5. El conductor 6. El/la dentista 7. El/la estudiante 8. El farmacéutico 9. El guardia 10. El/la turista. **2** 1. Car will not start. Town, by 5.00. 2. Lost car key. Railway station, by 3.00. 3. Puncture; can't find jack. Home, by 5.30.
3 • Tengo un pinchazo. • No puedo encontrar el gato. • Es el coche de mi amigo. • Gracias. • Sí, tengo que estar en el Hotel Sol a las seis. • Muchísimas gracias. Son ustedes muy amables.

UNIT 60 **1** (a) agua verde (b) agua mineral con cerveza (c) un partido de teatro (d) helado de queso (e) hace blanco. **2** 1. False. The flight number is 128. 2. True. 3. False. The flight number is 127 and the Gate is number 38. **3** a) ¿A qué hora sale el vuelo para Londres? b) ¿A qué hora sale el autobús para el centro de la ciudad? c) ¿A qué hora sale el taxi para el teatro? d) ¿A qué hora sale el tren para Toledo?

Grammar summary

Nouns, Articles and Gender

Nouns are masculine or feminine. Most masculine nouns end in **o**, and feminine nouns in **a**. 'The' is **el**, **los** with a masculine noun and **la**, **las** with a feminine noun. The plural is formed by adding **s** to a vowel and **es** to a consonant.

el libro, **los libros**	**la falda**, **las faldas**
el profesor, **los profesores**	**la mujer**, **las mujeres**

'A', 'an' is **un**, **unos** with masculine nouns and **una**, **unas** with a feminine.

un libro, **(unos) libros**	**una casa, (unas) casas**

(Words in brackets are rarely used, unless you are stressing 'some . . .'

Tengo unos amigos ingléses.	I have some English friends.

Adjectives

Those that end in **o** have four forms:

un vino blanco; **una casa blanca**; **vinos blancos**; **casas blancas**

Those that end in anything else have two forms:

un libro azul; **una blusa azul**; **libros azules**; **blusas azules**

Adjectives usually follow the noun. Adjectives of nationality which end in **o** are similar to **blanco**, and those that end in a consonant have four forms:

un chico español; **una chica española; chicos españoles**; **chicas españolas**

To compare things use **más ... que**.

Soy más alto que usted.	I'm taller than you.

'Better' is expressed by **mejor**.

El vino es mejor que el agua.	Wine is better than water.

Adverbs

To form an adverb, put **-mente** on the feminine form of the adjective: **Trabajo rápidamente**. 'I work quickly.'

Common irregular adverbs are: **bien**, 'well'; **mal**, 'badly'; **de prisa**, 'quickly'; **despacio**, 'slowly'; **temprano**, 'early'; **tarde**, 'late'.

Questions

(a) Use your voice and question marks:

Es inglés. He's English.	**¿Es inglés?** Is he English?

(b) Use **¿verdad?** or **¿no?**

Es inglés, ¿verdad?	He's English, isn't he?
Es inglés, ¿no?	He's English, isn't he?

(c) Use a question word.

¿Qué quiere usted?	What do you want?
¿Qué tiempo hace?	What's the weather like?
¿Qué tal?	How are you?
¿Qué tal el melón?	What's the melon like?
¿De qué color es?	What colour is it?
¿Dónde está el bar?	Where's the bar?
¿Adónde va usted?	Where are you going?
¿De dónde es?	Where's he from?
¿Cuánta fruta quiere?	How much fruit do you want?
¿Por qué bebe usted tanto?	Why do you drink so much?

Negatives

Use **no**. **No fumo**. 'I don't smoke.'
For 'nothing', use **nada**.

No tengo nada en el bolso.	I've got nothing in the bag.

Verbs

Regular verbs

There are three types of verb, referred to by the ending.

The present tense

	-ar **Comprar** (to buy)	**-er** **Comer** (to eat)	**-ir** **Vivir** (to live)
(yo)	**compro**	**como**	**vivo**
(tú)	**compras**	**comes**	**vives**
(él, ella)	**compra**	**come**	**vive**
(usted)	**compra**	**come**	**vive**
(nosotros/as)	**compramos**	**comemos**	**vivimos**
(vosotros/as)	**compráis**	**coméis**	**vivís**
(ellos/as)	**compran**	**comen**	**viven**
(ustedes)	**compran**	**comen**	**viven**

The simple past (preterite)

Used to refer to single actions in the past.

(yo)	**compré**	**comí**	**viví**
(tú)	**compraste**	**comiste**	**viviste**
(él, ella)	**compró**	**comió**	**vivió**
(usted)	**compró**	**comió**	**vivió**
(nosotros/as)	**compramos**	**comimos**	**vivimos**
(vosotros/as)	**comprasteis**	**comisteis**	**vivisteis**
(ellos/as)	**compraron**	**comieron**	**vivieron**
(ustedes)	**compraron**	**comieron**	**vivieron**

The imperfect

Used to refer to repeated actions (I used to ...) and descriptions in the past.

(yo)	**compraba**	**comía**	**vivía**
(tú)	**comprabas**	**comías**	**vivías**
(él, ella)	**compraba**	**comía**	**vivía**
(usted)	**compraba**	**comía**	**vivía**
(nosotros/as)	**comprábamos**	**comíamos**	**vivíamos**
(vosotros/as)	**comprabais**	**comíais**	**vivíais**
(ellos/as)	**compraban**	**comían**	**vivían**
(ustedes)	**compraban**	**comían**	**vivían**

Common irregular verbs

These do not follow the patterns given above, and must be learned separately.

	Ser 'to be' (permanently)	**Estar** 'to be' (temporarily)	**Ir** 'to go'
(yo)	**soy**	**estoy**	**voy**
(tú)	**eres**	**estás**	**vas**
(él, ella)	**es**	**está**	**va**
(usted)	**es**	**está**	**va**
(nosotros/as)	**somos**	**estamos**	**vamos**
(vosotros/as)	**sois**	**estáis**	**vais**
(ellos/as)	**son**	**están**	**van**
(ustedes)	**son**	**están**	**van**

(Pronouns in brackets are rarely used. **Usted** and **ustedes**, 'You' in polite speech, must be used.)

Stem-changing verbs

Verbs have a stem, and an ending: **pod + er = poder**. There are three types of these verbs:

	o/u changing to **ue**	**e** changing to **ie**,	**e** changing to **i** (**-ir** verbs only)
	Poder	**Empezar**	**Pedir**
	'to be able, can'	'to begin'	'to order, ask for'
(yo)	**puedo**	**empiezo**	**pido**
(tú)	**puedes**	**empiezas**	**pides**
(él, ella)	**puede**	**empieza**	**pide**
(usted)	**puede**	**empieza**	**pide**
(nosotros/as)	**podemos**	**empezamos**	**pedimos**
(vosotros/as)	**podéis**	**empezáis**	**pedís**
(ellos/as)	**pueden**	**empiezan**	**piden**
(ustedes)	**pueden**	**empiezan**	**piden**

Verbs with 1st person irregular forms

Coger	'to catch, take, seize'	**cojo**
Conocer	'to know'	**conozco**
Decir	'to say, tell'	**digo**
Hacer	'to make, do'	**hago**
Oír	'to hear'	**oigo**
Poner	'to put, place'	**pongo**
Saber	'to know'	**sé**
Salir	'to depart, leave, go out'	**salgo**
Tener	'to have'	**tengo**
Traer	'to bring'	**traigo**
Venir	'to come'	**vengo**

The imperative

The imperative is formed from the 1st person singular of the present tense. If this is irregular, so is the imperative.

Regular Verbs
Comprar – compro Remove the **o** and add **e**. **Compre pan**. 'Buy bread.'
Comer – como. Remove the **o** and add **a**. **Coma el pescado**. 'Eat the fish.'
Escribir – escribo. Remove the **o** and add **a**. **Escriba el precio**. 'Write the price.'

The only common Irregular Imperative is **ir**, 'to go'.
Ir – voy – *but* **vaya**. **Vaya al banco**. 'Go to the bank.'

Vocabulary

A

abierto/a open
la abuela the grandmother
el abuelo the grandfather
los abuelos the grandparents
aburrido/a boring
el aceite the oil
adiós goodbye
¿adónde? where to?
a eso de about (*of time*)
aficionado/a a keen on
agradable agreeable
el agua the water
ahí there
algo something, somewhat
¿algo más? anything further?
el algodón the cotton
alguno/a some
allí there
alquilar to hire, rent
alrededor de around
alto/a tall, high
la alumna the pupil
el ama de casa the housewife
amable pleasant, kind
amarillo/a yellow
la (el) amiga(o) the friend
el andén the platform
el anfiteatro the amphitheatre
antiguo/a old, ancient
el año the year
anunciar to announce
aparcar to park
apetecer to fancy
aquel that
aquí here
el árbol the tree
el armario the cupboard, wardrobe
arreglar to repair, arrange
asado/a roast
el autocar the coach
ayer yesterday
ayudar to help
azul blue

B

bajar to go down
bajo/a short (*in height*), low
el baño the bath
barato/a cheap
el barrio the district
bastante enough, rather
beber to drink
la bebida the drink
bien well
el billete the ticket (*travel*), note (*money*)
el bistec the steak
blanco/a white
el bocadillo sandwich, filled roll
la bodega the wine-cellar, drinks bill (*hotel*)
el bollo the bun
el bolso the handbag
'bomba' splendidly (*colloquial*)
bonito/a nice, pretty
el bonometro the special ticket for the Metro
la botella the bottle
bueno/a good
la bufanda the scarf
buscar to look for
la butaca the armchair, stall (*theatre, cinema*)

C

la cabeza the head
cada each, every
el café the coffee
la caja the cash-desk (*shop*)
la calle the street
el calor the heat
el camarero the waiter
cambiar to change
la camiseta the t-shirt
el campo the countryside
caro/a dear, expensive
la carretera the road
la casa the house
casado/a married
el castillo the castle
la cena the dinner
cerca (de) near (to)
el cerdo the pig, pork
la cerveza the beer
la charcutería the pork butcher's
el cheque de viaje the traveller's cheque
la chuleta the chop (*meat*)
el cine cinema
la cita the appointment, date

la ciudad the city
claro clear, light (*of colour*)
climatizado/a air-conditioned
el cobrador the conductor (*bus*)
el coche the car
la cocina the kitchen, cooking
coger to catch (*most meanings*)
el color the colour
el comedor the dining-room
comer to eat, have lunch
los comestibles the groceries
la comida the food, lunch
la comisaría the police-station
¿cómo? how, what?
cómodo/a comfortable
el compañero the companion
la compañía the company
completo/a full (*hotel, etc.*)
comprar to buy
las compras the shopping
comprender to understand
el comprimido the tablet (*medicine*)
comprobar to check, examine
con with
el conductor the driver
conmigo with me
conocer to know, be familiar with
Correos the Post Office
corriente ordinary, normal
corto/a short
la cosa the thing
costar to cost
creer to think, believe
la crema the cream
cruzar to cross
¿cuál? which?
cuando when
¿cuánto/a? how much
cuarenta forty
el cuarto the quarter
cuatro four
el cuchillo the knife
la cuenta the bill (*hotel, restaurant*)
la culpa the fault

D

dar to give
dar un paseo to go for a walk
de of, from
debajo (de) under
deber to have to, must, to owe
décimo/a tenth
delante (de) in front (of)
delgado/a slim, thin
dentro (de) within
denunciar to report (*crime, etc.*)
el departamento the compartment
el deporte the sport
deprisa quickly
derecha right
a la derecha on the right
derecho straight ahead
el desayuno the breakfast
desear to wish, desire
después (de) after
el detalle the detail
el día the day
diario/a daily
el dinero the money
la dirección the direction, address
directamente directly
el disco the record (*music*)
divertido/a amusing
doble double
doler to hurt
el dolor the pain
el domingo Sunday
¿dónde? where?
dormir to sleep
el dormitorio the bedroom
la ducha the shower
duro/a hard, difficult

E

emocionante exciting
empezar to begin
la empleada the (female) employee
el empleado the employee
encantador/a charming
encantar to love
encontrar to find, meet
enfrente (de) opposite
la ensalada the salad
en seguida at once
entonces then
la entrada the ticket, entrance
entre between
el equipo the team
el escaparate the shop window
escuchar to listen

ese/a that
eso es that's right
el español Spanish
los espárragos the asparagus
especial special
la esposa the wife
esquiar to ski
la estación de servicio the service station
la estación de ferrocarril the railway station
los Estados Unidos the United States
estar to be
este/a this
el este the east
el estofado the stew
estudiar to study
estupendo/a marvellous
exactamente exactly
extranjero/a foreign

F

fabricar to make, manufacture
el farmacéutico the chemist
el faro the headlight
el favor the favour
la feria the fair
el fin the end
el final the end (*of street*)
firmar to sign
el flan the caramel custard
el francés French
la fresa the strawberry
el frío the cold
la fritura the fried dish
la fruta the fruit
funcionar to work (*machines*)

G

las gafas de sol the sunglasses
la ganga the bargain
la garganta the throat
el gato the cat, jack (*for car*)
el gazpacho the cold soup
la gente the people
gordo/a fat
gracias thank you
el grado the degree (*of heat, etc.*)
grande big
gratis free
greco Greek (*archaic*)
gris grey
guapo/a pretty (*people*)
el/la guía the guide
gustar to please

H

la habitación the room
el/la habitante the inhabitant
hablar to speak
hacer to do, make
hasta until, as far as
hay there is, there are
hecho done (*of meat*)
el helado the ice-cream
la hermana the sister
el hermano the brother
la hija the daughter
el hijo the son
histórico/a historical
el hombre the man
la hora the hour, time
hoy today

I

la ida single, journey
el idioma the language
Inglaterra England
el inglés the Englishman, English
la inglesa the English woman, girl
la insolación the sun stroke
interesante interesting
el invierno the winter
ir to go
izquierdo/a left
a la izquierda on the left

J

el jamón the ham
el jardín the garden
la jarra the jug
jubilado/a retired
jueves Thursday
jugar to play (*games*)

L

la you (*female pronoun*)
el lado the side
el ladrón the thief
el lago the lake
largo/a long
la lástima the pity, shame
el lavaplatos the dishwasher

la lechuga the lettuce
leer to read
lejos (de) far (from)
levantarse to get up
la libra the pound (*money*)
libre free
el libro the book
la liga the league
limpiar to clean
limpio/a clean
listo/a ready
llamarse to be called
la llave the key
la llegada the arrival
llegar to arrive
llevar to wear, take
llover to rain
loco/a mad, insane
luego then, next
lunes Monday

M

la madre the mother
mal badly
la maleta the suitcase
el maletero the boot (*car*), trunk
mandar to send
la manera the way, manner
la manga the sleeve
la mano the hand
la manzana the apple
mañana tomorrow
el mañana (the) tomorrow, the future
la mañana the morning
el mapa the map
la marca the brand, make
el marido the husband
marrón brown
martes Tuesday
más more
mayor larger, greater, elder
me me, myself
la media the half
mejor better
el melocotón the peach
el melón the melon
menos less
el mercado the market
la mesa the table
mi my
miércoles Wednesday
mil one thousand
mirar to look at
la misa the Mass
la molestia the trouble, bother
la moto the motorcycle
mucho/a much, a lot
la muela the tooth, molar
la muralla the city wall
el museo the museum

N

nada nothing
nadar to swim
la naranjada the orangeade
la nata the cream
negro/a black
el neumático the tyre
nevar to snow
la nevera the refrigerator
la noche the night
el nombre the name
el norte the north
el norteamericano the North American
noveno/a ninth
el número the number

O

o or
octavo/a eighth
ocurrir to occur, happen
el oeste the west
oír to hear
el ojo the eye
el ordenador the computer
otro/a another

P

el padre the father
pagar to pay
el país the country
el pan the bread
el panecillo the bread roll
los pantalones the trousers
para for, destined for
el parachoques the bumper, fender
la parada the stop (*bus, taxis*)
parecer to seem, appear
el partido the match, game
partir to share, to set off
  a partir de from

pasado/a last
pasarlo bien to enjoy oneself
el pasatiempo the pastime
la patata the potato
el pedido the order (*business*)
pedir to ask for, order
la película the film
peligroso/a dangerous
el pelo the hair
pensar to think
pequeño/a small
la pera the pear
perdido/a lost
el perdón the forgiveness, pardon
perdón excuse me
perdonar to forgive
permitir to allow, permit
pero but
persona mayor old person
el pescado fish
el pie the foot
la piel the leather
el pinchazo the puncture
la piscina the swimming pool
el piso the flat, floor
el plátano the banana
el plato the dish, plate
la playa the beach
la plaza the square
el plomo the lead
poder to be able, can
el pollo the chicken
poner to put
por for, through, along
porque because
¿por qué? why?
el postre the dessert
practicar to play (*games*)
preguntar to ask
preocuparse to worry
primero/a first
prisa hurry
  deprisa quickly
tener prisa to be in a hurry
probarse to try on (*clothes*)
el procesador de textos the word processor
el profesor the teacher
la profesora the (woman) teacher
próximo/a next
el pueblo the village
la puerta the door, city gate
el puesto the stall (*in market*)

Q

¿qué? what?
¡qué! what a … how …!
quedar to stay, remain
las quemaduras del sol the sunburn
querer to wish, want, love
el queso the cheese
¿quién? who?
quinto/a fifth
el quiosco the kiosk

R

recibir to receive
el recibo the receipt
el recuerdo the souvenir, memory
recuerdos a … regards to …
la red the network, net
el revisor the ticket collector
el río the river
robar to rob
el robo the theft
rojo/a red
la ropa the clothing
roto/a broken
la rueda de recambio the spare wheel
la ruta the route

S

sábado Saturday
la sábana the sheet
saber to know (*facts*), to know how to
sacar to take out, obtain
sacar fotos to take photographs
la salida the departure, exit
el salón lounge
salir to go out, leave, depart
el salón lounge
la sed the thirst
segundo/a second
el seguro the insurance
el sello the postage stamp
la semana the week
sentarse to sit down
sentir to feel
el señor the gentleman, Mr
la señorita the young lady, Miss
la señora the lady, Mrs

séptimo/a seventh
ser to be
servir to serve, help
sexto/a sixth
si if
sí yes
siempre always
la sierra the mountain range
el siglo the century
significar to mean, signify
la silla the chair
simpático/a nice, pleasant (*people*)
sin without
el sol the sun
soler to usually do
sólo only
su his, her, your, their
subir to go up
sucio/a dirty
la suerte good luck
súper 4-star, high grade (petrol)
el sur the south

T

la talla the size (*clothing*)
también also
tanto/a so much, so many
el taquillero the ticket-seller
tardarse en to take time
la tarde the afternoon, evening
la tarjeta de crédito the credit card
la tarjeta postal the postcard
la tarta helada the ice-cream cake
te you, yourself
la tela the cloth, fabric
el tenedor the fork
tener to have, own
el tiempo the weather, time
la tía the aunt
la tienda de modas the dress shop
tinto red (*wine*)
el tío the uncle
la toalla the towel
todo/a all
tomar to take, have (*food and drink*)
tomar el sol to sunbathe
torcer to twist, turn
la tortilla the omelette
trabajar to work
el trabajo the work, job
traer to bring
el/la transeúnte the passerby
el tren the train
tu your
el tubo the tube

U

único/a only (*child*)
unos/as some
usted you
la uva the grape

V

las vacaciones the holidays
valer to be worth, cost
varios/as several
el vaso the glass
vender to sell
venir to come
la ventanilla the window (*car*), counter, cash desk (*bank, etc.*)
ver to see
el verano the summer
¿verdad? true?
verde green
la verdulería the greengrocer's
el vestido the dress
vestirse to dress
la vía the track (*railways*)
viajar to travel
el viaje the journey
el viajero the traveller
la viajera the traveller (*female*)
la vida the life
el viento the wind
viernes Friday
el vino the wine
vivir to live
volver to return
el vuelo the flight

Grammar and Topic Indexes

Numbers refer to units.